WORK
SMART
NOW

WORK
SMART
NOW

HOW TO JUMP START PRODUCTIVITY, EMPOWER EMPLOYEES, AND ACHIEVE MORE

RICHARD POLAK

Skyhorse Publishing

Skyhorse Publishing books may be purchased in bulk at special discounts for sales promotion, corporate gifts, fund-raising, or educational purposes. Special editions can also be created to specifications. For details, contact the Special Sales Department, Skyhorse Publishing, 307 West 36th Street, 11th Floor, New York, NY 10018 or info@skyhorsepublishing.com.

Skyhorse® and Skyhorse Publishing® are registered trademarks of Skyhorse Publishing, Inc.®, a Delaware corporation.

Visit our website at www.skyhorsepublishing.com.

10 9 8 7 6 5 4 3 2 1

Library of Congress Cataloging-in-Publication Data

Names: Polak, Richard (Human resource veteran) author.
Title: Work smart now: how to jump-start productivity, empower employees, and achieve more / Richard Polak.
Description: New York, NY: Skyhorse Publishing, [2021] | Includes
    bibliographical references and index. | Identifiers: LCCN 2020057017 (print) |
LCCN 2020057018 (ebook) | ISBN
    9781510759824 (hardcover) | ISBN 9781510759831 (ebook)
Subjects: LCSH: Time management. | Wages and labor productivity. |
    Work-life balance. | Job stress.
Classification: LCC HD69.T54 P63 2021 (print) | LCC HD69.T54 (ebook) |
    DDC 650.1/1cdc23
LC record available at https://lccn.loc.gov/2020057017
LC ebook record available at https://lccn.loc.gov/2020057018

Cover design by Daniel Brount

Print ISBN: 978-1-5107-5982-4
Ebook ISBN: 978-1-5107-5983-1

Printed in the United States of America

Contents

Preface

Time is our second-greatest asset. We all run out of it eventually, so we need to use it wisely. Whether it's in the office or in the living room, none of us are getting the most out of the time we've been given. From the moment we wake up and check our Facebook page or emails—before we even crawl out of bed—to late at night when we stay up longer than we should, watching TV or working. From the government worker in Cairo who averages 10 to 20 percent less productivity a day (according to many studies) to the salesperson in Cincinnati who takes an extended lunch, has trivial chitchat with his or her coworker, and checks his or her email too often (studies show that it is more productive to check your email only twice a day). Lack of productivity, which extends to lack of engagement, is a crisis in much of society. Workers are pushed beyond their limits. This is proven by studies that show increased dissatisfaction at work and higher rates of depression and suicide. It's simply bad business to overwork people. People become less productive and companies lose money and risk losing employees. In America alone, the average business loses 10 to 25 percent in revenue due to this phenomenon. It's only now that we are able to measure it, analyze it, and make changes.

For more than 40 years, I've been advising organizations around the world. For most of that time, I owned and operated one of the largest privately held global consultancies, advising companies such as Google, Sony Pictures, Hilton Hotels, and McDonald's on international expansion and productivity in more than 90 countries. I became the specialist, flying around the world, building bridges between employees and their employers through innovative human resources (HR) tools that brought the two groups together. I became an HR forensics investigator, hired by numerous companies to uncover rogue employees who were stealing money from the company and breaking numerous laws in the country. Some were just flat-out mobsters. My goal, as directed by the CEOs, was to stop the corruption immediately and prevent the news from landing on the front page of the *New York Times*. I'm pleased to report that not one of my clients ever ended up in the news concerning these sensitive issues.

I have learned valuable tools that I utilize in my personal business as well as advise for the businesses of others. Here are my two definitions of productivity:

"Get More Done in Less Time—and Do It with Joy"
"Do Only the Things That Only You Can Do."

Previous generations said, "Work Harder," but now we've learned it really is "Work Smarter." I have successfully tested my methods in hundreds of opportunities. Every individual and business should have these tools.

This is why I wrote *Work Smart Now,* to condense many decades of knowledge into an easy-to-read book that every top-performing individual, CEO, or high-level executive can refer to for guidance.

I hope this book is helpful to you. It has certainly been a joy to write, and the lessons contained herein have been helpful to me in making my whole life more productive.

It is written in somewhat of an unorthodox style. You'll notice that I begin each chapter with a bit of dialogue, as a stage play is written. This is because, frankly, it is my most comfortable form of writing (I've had seven plays produced and published by Samuel French). I understand that writing a book is not the same, but I truly hope this format works for you. It certainly made it more fun and interesting for me to write this way, and I wanted to do so only to get my vision across to you.

So, if time is our second-greatest asset, what is our first? It's our integrity. You can have all the time in the world, but without integrity you have nothing.

—Richard Polak

CHAPTER ONE

The Coffee Klatch
and Research
(There Is Science Involved)

Our story opens in the conference room of the CEO. This room has a rich feel. Centered is a mahogany conference table—not a scratch on it. Sitting around the table are three employees, all well-dressed (but no suits or ties—business casual). Three employees are on the screen calling in from their home offices. The room is replete with modern technology and state-of-the-art communication tools: large monitors on both walls, HD cameras, and more. Big business is conducted in this room. If the room could talk, it would say "success."

CEO: Hello, everyone. It's good to see you. Thank you all for attending this coffee klatch. Does anybody have any idea why I've asked you to join me? (pause from the group)

CEO: There is no wrong answer.

Bethany: We're all getting raises?

CEO: (pause) I love your sense of humor.
(some soft laughter)

Bethany: We're all getting fired.

CEO: Wrong answer again. Bethany, these are extremes. I wonder what's going on with your work . . . just kidding.

Kent: Some of us are getting fired?

CEO: Well, I can see this is going to be fun. I've asked you all to join me today so I can receive honest feedback about an initiative I plan to launch. I know it might sound odd that the CEO wants honest feedback, but it's true. I need it. I can't help the organization or yourselves if I don't get honest feedback.

Milton: Why us?

CEO: You are each leaders in your area.

Kent: (inflating his chest) Yes, I guess we are.

Bethany: Is the company doing okay?

CEO: The company is doing fine. But fine is not good enough—not for me, and it shouldn't be for you either. I want us to improve. Essentially, this is and should be the same mission for every corporation. My job is to do the best I can for everyone with a vested interest in the company, its stakeholders, and its shareholders. And while you might or might not be shareholders, I consider you stakeholders. You all come from different departments: marketing, sales, operations, finance, and administration. That's by design. I want a balanced perspective on my plans and how they might impact different parts of the organization. Any questions?

(no questions)

CEO: Everything we talk about here today and in future coffee klatches—if you agree to attend—will remain confidential. I might take action based on the feedback I receive from you, but nobody's name will be used in the process except in a positive light if I feel that would help you and the company.

(Attendees in the room are appropriately respectful, listening, some fidgeting due to nerves)

CEO: Now, what I plan to do today is to take us all on a journey.

Kent: (excited) Hawaii?

CEO: A personal journey. A corporation looking to grow has two choices: increase revenue or decrease costs in order to make more profit. Remember, profits are good for everybody, including the employees, because profits will be shared with everyone. The journey I hope to take us on will increase revenue rather than cut costs. Cutting costs ultimately leads to less business, unhappy employees, and disengagement. It's better to increase profits by increasing revenue. To do this compassionately, however, we must increase productivity. Now, that does not mean working harder. Not necessarily. Take a look at this chart.

(The CEO hands out the following chart.)

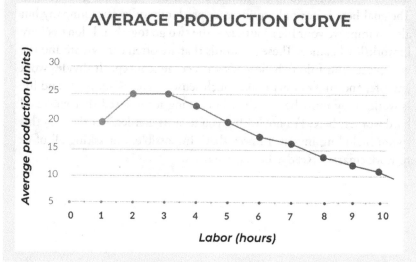

CEO: You can see that working harder doesn't necessarily produce better results. It literally means just working harder. Working harder is important, but working smarter is even more important. Any questions so far?

Bethany: Can you elaborate further on how we can increase productivity without working harder? I'm not quite getting that. I see from the chart that it's optimal to work two or three hours.

CEO: Yes, that's true. This is a general chart of productivity. If you were on an assembly line, you could work longer and still be productive. However, if you're in professional services, two to three hours without a break is your maximum. We're going to discuss this and many other topics during our journey together. It'll take time for the company to make changes. In this session, first I'll show you the data and research that supports what I plan to roll out. Hopefully, I will gain consensus. Second, I'll talk about all the productivity buckets: absenteeism/presenteeism, well-being, engagement, technology, and, finally, optimizing your own workday and, by extension, improving your lives. It's the combination of all these together that will make an impact. We have a wellness program. We have some initiatives on engagement, but they are not measured or coordinated together to produce great results. The goal here is not only to increase productivity in our company but also to improve your life's journey—the two go together. I don't believe in work/life balance. These are words that are often thrown around the workplace, and I don't believe it's an accurate concept. It divides work and life, and that doesn't make much sense to me. Work is life and life is work. They must be together. I'm taking for granted that you're all hard workers here. I'm not asking you to work harder. For those in this room, including myself, I know that's impossible. I'm asking all of us to work smarter. Ready? Let's get started.

There is a preponderance of research on how increased productivity improves results in an organization and, more importantly, improves results in the lives of its employees. So, there is a way to actually have your cake and eat it, too.

Throughout this book, I will show you documented research I have gathered from a myriad of sources. This supports everything I've learned through my experience.

You may look only at the "sound bites" and move on, and there's nothing wrong with that. I wanted to show you the amount of research because it's indisputable—human nature does not change. Our great philosophers (who I refer to as the first HR professionals) Plato, Aristotle, Nietzsche, and many more, are long gone, but the principles they established regarding human behavior are the same. As I publish further editions of this book, I will only add to this research list.

Another thing to note about research: follow the money. Some research is driven by self-interest. Some of what you will see is essentially hidden behind sophisticated advertising and promotion. For example, a wellness company doing its own survey on wellness is not credible. After all, would you publish findings that don't implicitly back up the product that is your livelihood, or would you ensure that the results make your product necessary? This same principle holds true with insurance companies, recruiters, consultants, and others. Even research by academic institutions is often funded by self-interest groups. With that in mind, I've tried to include the most credible sources possible. It's not an exhaustive collection, but as I said, collectively it's indisputable.

The Financial Impact

Duke University conducted a study that lasted about five years. The study observed and analyzed the impact of work on the health and wellness of 6,700 employees who came from a range of corporations in unrelated fields. Research showed that 60 percent of people were stressed or overwhelmed by financial obligations even though they worked for a living wage. Furthermore, only half of those companies offered financial education programs to help alleviate these concerns. The Federal Reserve Board estimates that financial stress among employees costs the employees' companies $5,000 per employee per year in lost productivity (higher turnover, absenteeism, presenteeism). If you have 1,000 employees, that's $5,000,000 off the bottom line.

The fact that this book must be written is somewhat beyond me. The thought that the lack of productivity has been lurking in corporations' backyards for decades and has not been addressed appropriately is astonishing because fixing the issue is really one of the easiest ways to make money. I think this has not come to light earlier only because of the lack of creativity in many CEOs. It's easier to follow prescriptive business school formulas to make money—pressure people to work harder, cut costs, and risk forcing sales on products that are inferior for your customers—but it makes more business sense to encourage compassionate productivity. Empower employees to do better. All the research supports the wisdom of this approach.

Great workplaces have 65 percent less turnover and five times higher stock market returns than industry peers. They also have higher earnings per share, outperforming those peers by 202 percent.[*]

At my first job, I learned a hard lesson on how business works. I always gave to charities, and I saw that companies do so, too. When I was in my early 20s, I approached the CEO of the company I was working for and asked if we could donate to a special homeless organization. He asked me who was on the board of directors of the organization. I said I didn't know, but that it was an important organization that helped a lot of people. He leaned toward me and said (I'm paraphrasing), "Richard, we are a business. We're happy to give to charities if it will further our business interests. For example, if you knew someone on the board that we do business with or could potentially do business with, we could justify a contribution. Otherwise, the business cannot support it." This was eye-opening to me . . . and very sad. On the other hand, it taught me an important lesson about business. I needed to find creative ways to give to society under the aegis of being "good for business." What I did for one firm in Germany, a giant multinational where the executive team did not want to provide a pension plan for its German employees, was to show that the profits would increase due to the boost in productivity by employees receiving a pension plan. In addition, if they looked at the benchmarking data of what the company's competitors were doing, a pension plan for the employees was essential to

---

*   Source: *Corporate Culture and Performance* by J. P. Kotter & J. L. Heskett; Great Places to Work® Institute; and Deloitte's "Culture in the Workplace"; Gallup (2016) State of the Global Workplace; The Relationship Between Engagement at Work and Organizational Outcomes: Gallup.

attracting and retaining talent. This combination presented the business case for a pension plan for the employees in Germany. It all worked out fine, and to this day these German employees are able to retire with dignity after a 35-year career with the company.

There must be an "in-between" state that exists to separate dispassionate business growth with an eye on overworked employees suffering from burnout. The result of burnout is a drop in morale from unreasonable expectations resulting in a loss of productivity. The answer to balancing "good business practices"—those that generally result in increased profits and lower costs—with human needs and emotions is compassionate productivity, and it can be an absolute game changer.

What Is Compassionate Productivity?

Compassionate productivity is the idea that recognizing employees as human beings with their own struggles, triumphs, goals, and motivations results in better overall work. This isn't something that should be new to business, and to be fair, it's not completely unused in certain industries. In general, however, organizational decision makers tend to favor a more hard-edged approach that emphasizes strictly separating the human from their work. This is a mistake for a few different reasons, all of which we'll examine in sections that follow.

Before we move on, however, it should be noted that compassionate productivity isn't an extreme. We aren't looking at a situation where one end of the spectrum is the concept that employees must be extrinsically motivated—be it by stress or by other means—in order to work as well as they can and where the other end is compassionate productivity. The idea of compassionate productivity is actually a happy medium between two extremes: the aforementioned perspective that sees employees as a means to an end to be "motivated" in whatever manner necessary, and one that allows employees to work however and whenever they want.

It is possible to give employees the space they need to thrive without also compromising on the business processes that you know work for your organization. And when you get that balance just right, you might be surprised at how much the productivity of your workforce improves as your workers show what they can achieve when they are happy and passionate about their jobs.

In the following chapters for the CEO and management, we will take a look at some of the components that are vital to boosting productivity and helping employees reach their full potential. For the employee, in reading this, it will inform you on how to excel in the organization. But before we move forward, I want to talk about building a workplace culture that promotes compassion and understanding over fears and threats to lower performance reviews before we get there. This is a fundamental idea that should serve as the foundation for the rest of the tips and lessons in this book—a strong base upon which you can create the environment that is perfect for your business and the workforce.

Compassionate Productivity Versus Traditional Performance Incentives

Traditionally, improving workplace performance has been accomplished by setting goals and pushing employees to meet them by whatever means necessary. According to Emma Seppala, associate director of the Stanford University Center for Compassion and Altruism Research and Education, the most common motivator in the past was a reprimand—part of a checks-and-balances system that served to remind employees that their jobs were entirely dependent upon their performance and that any deviation from an upward trajectory might cost them their career.[*] This had the added "benefit" of projecting the potential consequences of underperforming or mistakes to the rest of the department or team, too. Keeping everyone "on their toes" was the preferred way to drive productivity and performance—in other words, by instilling fear and stress into the workforce.

Whereas this method has long been the go-to method in many industries, today's research shows that it is not the best way to go about motivating employees to do better. In one study published in the *Journal of Management*, for example, researchers found that the focus on achievements above all else only leads to workaholism and increased stress levels, both of which actually serve to hinder productivity and diminish work quality, rather than improve

---

[*]   Parker, C., 2015. Compassion Is a Wise And Effective Managerial Strategy, Stanford Expert Says | Stanford News Release. [online] News.stanford.edu. Available at: <https://news.stanford.edu /pr/2015/pr-compassion-workplace-seppala-052115.html>.

it.* And while pushing employees to work harder and longer hours in order to meet a specific goal or deadline might not result in "true" workaholism—that is, the compulsion to work as much as possible despite negative consequences in personal relationships or other out-of-work experiences and connections— it results in very similar behavior. Instead of being internally motivated to work despite an overall decrease in quality of life, focusing on achievements and meeting quotas tends to result in "workaholism" born from the fear of losing an income or damaging a career. Despite the difference in motivators, the end results are much the same.

As the study notes, workaholism is tied to negative outcomes. These include job stress, burnout, poorer mental and physical health, and work/life conflict. In later chapters, we'll see exactly how each of these factors negatively impacts productivity, but suffice to say that they do nothing to improve the long-term productivity of employees. Eventually, constant fear and stress will cause almost everyone to experience burnout and apathy. That might manifest directly in the workplace itself, or it might be something that occurs mostly in the employee's personal life. But, regardless, the negative impact of these factors on motivation and productivity are the same.

More specifically, Seppala notes—and I agree—that traditional approaches to incentivizing performance boosts in the workplace result in high stress levels that often disrupt an organization's culture. This is a problem. First, and perhaps most practically in the short term, individuals operating from fear and stress are less able to reason and think clearly, something that naturally results in a drop in work performance. In the long term, a disruption in corporate culture can cause many cracks to form and widen in an organization's overall mission as well as in the unity of its workforce as a whole. The goal is to create an organization with employees who believe in their work and the company's overall vision. That unity helps boost worker morale as well as productivity. When the workforce is highly stressed and is more concerned about getting work done than about completing quality work with the well-being of the organization in mind, that workforce begins to fracture. And a fractured workforce produces a far less effective workplace.

---

*   Clark, M., Michel, J., Zhdanova, L., Pui, S. and Baltes, B., 2016. All Work and No Play? A Meta-Analytic Examination of the Correlates and Outcomes of Workaholism. *Journal of Management*, 42(7): 1836–1873.

The increased stress and fear encouraged by traditional performance incentives also discourage innovation. When your employees are fully aware that any mistake could "land them in hot water," they will become less and less willing to take risks. Instead of encouraging the workforce to think outside the box in order to boost performance and work quality, this kind of approach serves only to diminish autonomy and reduce confidence and decision making. Employees will favor tried-and-true methods and will avoid going out on a limb, ensuring that the organization maintains the status quo for as long as possible rather than thriving or reinventing itself. And while maintaining "good enough" right now might sound acceptable, most organizations will see the error of their ways a few years down the road. The world is changing quickly and dramatically. Businesses unable or unwilling to embrace innovation are doomed to slowly stagnate and fade away.

Finally, pushing employees to work as hard as possible with no regard for their well-being will lower their passion. And when they are punished for mistakes they likely made out of fear while attempting to meet a certain deadline, their loyalty and trust will also quickly diminish. That's a serious problem because turnover can have lasting effects on an organization's workforce as a whole. Missing an experienced and capable team member impacts everyone, not just immediate coworkers. If this situation is a repeating one, then departments will likely find themselves rarely operating at their full potential simply because their employees either are new to the organization or are already on the way out and searching for new positions.

The much better alternative to traditional performance-based incentives is compassionate productivity. This approach, as further explained by Seppala, is rooted in the idea that reaching out to employees from a place of compassion is much more effective at promoting long-term productivity and high-quality work. First of all, employees who are shown compassion and understanding even when they've made a mistake of some kind are much more likely to begin to trust their employers. Trusting in employers leads to loyalty and dedication, both of which are vital to a successful organization that thrives for the foreseeable future regardless of the changes that await it in the process. Loyal employees do more than just show up. They make every moment of their workday count and do their best to produce quality work that benefits their company and their coworkers.

None of this means that mistakes go unnoticed or that employees never face consequences for their actions. Mistakes and missed deadlines aren't something to be encouraged, and it is important to have clear expectations for employees to meet. The compassion comes from how you approach even unpleasant conversations, not from whether or not employees experience negative consequences or take a hit to their performance reviews. There is a significant difference between asking an employee what happened— empathizing with that employee about the circumstances that led them to the error and giving them the tools they need to do better, along with a warning—and simply chastising them for not doing as well as you believe they should be doing, without exhibiting any kind of concern or compassion for their well-being. The latter will only breed fear and distrust; the former, even when the employees face negative consequences, will dramatically lessen any anger or sense of injustice they experience.

Traditional perspectives regarding employees, and how to motivate them or address areas of concern, ultimately break down their drive and their belief that they can do a good job. They erode autonomy—that is, fear encourages employees to make repetitive choices rather than ones that might result in the best possible work, building apathy and burnout in the process. Showing compassion results in an employee who understands where they made a mistake and how to avoid making another one—it results in employees who have learned to do better and be more effective at their jobs without feeling demoralized in the process. This is an important distinction that makes a world of difference. Keep in mind that employees who learn from their errors via managers or overseers who show them compassion and kindness are more likely to *want* to do better in order to repay the concern shown to them.

How to Practice Compassion in the Workplace

Understanding the concept of compassionate productivity is important but being able to establish the practice is even more important. Keep in mind as you move forward to give your employees the best chance possible at reaching their full potential and boosting workplace productivity and happiness. These are not the only things to keep in mind, of course, and you might find that different approaches fit your business and your employees better than others—and that's okay. In fact, that's one of the most important guidelines to remember as you move through this book. Not everything will work for everyone exactly as described, but there is usually some kind of compromise that can be made to combine innovation in productivity with current business practices.

With that said, the first step to offering compassionate productivity is to be mindful. This is something many of us could benefit from, even in our personal lives, much less in the workplace. Before you speak or act, take a moment and gather your thoughts and your emotions. The last thing you want to do is speak from a place of anger or frustration, and it is imperative to allow your immediate instinct to fade before approaching the employee(s) in question. Think about what you want to say before you say it. Consider making notes on the key points that must be addressed and bring them with you in order to keep yourself on track and avoid going off on a tangent. Finally, breathing exercises and meditation take only a few moments to work and either of them (or both, if you'd prefer) will help you to act from a place of mindfulness while keeping your emotions regulated.

The next step is to keep empathy firmly in mind at all times. You know how you feel and why you feel that way, but you don't truly understand how your employee feels or what led them to feel that way—you simply couldn't unless you'd lived their whole life. It's important not only to express the reasoning behind your emotions and your expectations but also to listen to, and respect, what your employees have to say. They will all have different experiences and factors that impact their behavior and their performance, from anxiety to family issues to an unreasonably high workload. Find out what is going on and how you can adjust your mindset or give your employee tips to adjust theirs in order to help them find success. Once again, there is almost always a compromise to be made between what you want to do in order to preserve your bottom line and what will most benefit your employee, your workforce, and your organization overall. Understand where your employees are coming from before you say too much.

Finally, practice forgiveness. Employees rarely make mistakes out of spite alone—there is usually another factor that leads to the issues in question. Don't take their actions personally, because it is unlikely that they acted with the intention to harm you or the company. Not only will practicing forgiveness help you achieve mindfulness and empathy, but it will also help reduce your own stress. This is an important and often ignored benefit. Your organization needs strong, effective leaders in order to thrive. You can't be on the front lines if you are burned out or demoralized yourself. Take the time to forgive and move forward, for your own sake as well as for your employee's.

These are a few initial things you can do in order to practice compassionate productivity. It's important to keep in mind that this approach works best in a workplace culture that has been designed to support it. You can be as compassionate as you want in individual interactions but will be unlikely to reap many benefits if your organization's culture in general emphasizes performance above all else. Keep expectations and empathy standardized in all aspects of your business and enable your employees to feel appreciated in everything they do. In other words, create an amazing workplace that promotes happiness, productivity, and innovation at every level, and you are sure to see a big difference in how your workforce functions. Not sure how to create that kind of workplace? That's okay—we'll talk about it a bit more in the next chapter.

With the understanding that business is about making money, promoting compassionate productivity can and will deliver results. In the end, it's about money. That's the reality. We can do good, much good, but the money has to follow. So with the amount of money at stake—you'll see exactly how much we're talking about a bit later—I am astonished, even shocked, that major corporations do not have a director of productivity and a staff dedicated to increasing productivity. One would think that because there's so much money to be gained, companies would be putting much more effort into this initiative. Perhaps there just wasn't enough evidence to sway them—until now. Let's move on and see how this unfolds.

The Business Case

What you'll see in upcoming chapters is the business case for implementing changes in your organization. This will include numbers your CFO will need in order to justify the expense of an investment in productivity gains. I've worked with many CFOs over my career. They are trained to look at numbers. If the numbers don't support an investment, then the company shouldn't make it—it's really quite simple for them. And, truthfully, it makes sense. The business fundamentals are based on numbers; the CEO would agree. No one will make an investment unless they can see the return on investment (ROI). Sometimes, for example, when I was working in mergers and acquisitions (M&A), there would be a reason to buy a firm for goodwill or technology. The ROI wasn't evident or there wasn't a clear, set number. Well, that's rare and that's not what I'm going to present in this book. In this book, you'll see hard numbers that will benefit the organization by making important productivity changes. The numbers you'll see in the "Business Case" section of this book are unique because they don't even consider the value added in improving the lives of the employees and the branding of the company. Those are values that are hard to put a number on. In fact, what value can you put on improving someone's life? You can't. It's priceless.

CHAPTER TWO

Introducing Productivity (Modern-Day Techniques for the Modern-Day Company)

CEO: Thank you all for attending once again. When we last met, we discussed all the research that supports the productivity initiative I plan to roll out. These improvements will help the firm without stressing individuals. In fact, the initiative is designed to relieve pressure rather than add to it.

Bethany: How?

CEO: Well, let's take a look. Picture three circles, a small circle inside a medium-sized one, inside a larger one. The inner circle represents **Comfort**. The second circle represents **Discomfort**. The third circle represents **Panic**. Does anybody have an idea where I'm going with this?

Bethany: I'll take a guess.

CEO: Great. Go ahead.

Bethany: You want us in the comfort zone.

CEO: Nope.

Bethany: Panic zone?

CEO: Nope.

Bill: You want us to be uncomfortable because we can't grow or learn if we're comfortable or panicked.

CEO: Exactly. That's a means to live your personal lives too. If you're not challenged, you will not grow. Life isn't stagnant. No matter how hard one might try, one cannot stay the same. If you do nothing to grow and learn, you won't stay the same—you will regress. You will actually slow down, atrophy, and deteriorate. You will be less happy. We all must be on a growth path. This company—any corporation, really—manifests that with growth. I've always thought that business was an excuse for people to connect and grow. I'm hoping on a much higher level that I'll be able to achieve this within the company. But it cannot be done without growing financially. They go hand in hand. At the very core, for those in this room, especially professional services folks, change "Do only the things that you can do," to "Only do the things that only you can do." Everything else should be discarded or delegated.

Definition of Productivity

For the purposes of this book, we are using the term *productivity* in the context of individuals—in some cases, team performance. The OECD, World Bank, United Nations, and other governmental and nongovernmental organizations use the term as a ratio between the output volume and the volume of inputs. One of the most widely used measures of productivity is gross domestic product (GDP) per hour worked. In the previous chapter, I mentioned this as an important marker. However, note that hours worked does not necessarily translate to a great GDP. The same concept applies in your organization. Remember, top performers don't necessarily work harder. They work smarter. If they work smart and hard, they'll achieve optimal performance. The emphasis here is not on "hard," it's on "smart." I think we all work hard. Our corporations and enterprises have pushed that concept to the limit. This is clear from all the research showing stress levels of individuals around the world.

Fundamentals

Before we dig into this chapter, it's important to emphasize that there are fundamentals that a company must achieve before this book and its precepts can make an impact. Increasing productivity is not an excuse for bad fundamentals. Even if your firm is perceived as currently running well, the company must have the basic fundamentals in order to optimize productivity. This book is designed to add value to an existing organization that is already healthy. First, you must get your house in order with the very basic tenets of running a business: financial, sales, marketing, and operations. This goes for your personal lives as well. You must have the foundation of a reasonably healthy life in order to build a healthy business, and that primarily includes both physical and mental health.

The truth is that there are many different factors that influence how well a workplace runs and how that impacts its workforce. Without a fundamentally sound workplace and culture, it will be almost impossible to take steps to maximize productivity and worker potential. And despite the research available on the topic, it turns out that creating a great workplace is a bit less common than it should be. With that in mind, I want to talk about how to define a great workplace and what you should think about as you look at bettering your own. Don't assume that you have it under control or that your current workplace "works" just fine. There is a difference between thriving and surviving, and shouldn't you want your business to fall under the former? So, let's talk about how you can create an office that promotes growth and innovation.

What Defines a Great Workplace?

What is a "great" workplace? Many might believe that organizations offering the best benefits, such as healthcare and free meals, automatically create the best office environments, but that's not necessarily true. While things like complimentary food and comprehensive healthcare are important to overall workforce health and happiness, they alone do not determine whether a workplace is objectively "great." A truly great workplace is one where employees are valued as individuals and where differences not only are accepted but also are embraced as opportunities to better the overall work experience. Diversity is something to be appreciated in these offices because it helps the organization in question understand many different viewpoints and create better overall products or services in response. A great workplace also offers straightforward, honest information to its employees rather than anything that is spun or suppressed, while also adding value to them. Rather than being perceived as a replaceable means to an end, workers in these spaces are seen as valuable to the organization and are treated with dignity and respect with that truth in mind. Finally, great workplaces offer their employees something to be passionate about, from rewarding work to a meaningful mission and value statement. Employees want to feel as though their efforts are contributing to a greater good, and great organizations make sure that their employees understand exactly how they're helping.

Many of these factors might not seem out of the ordinary. In fact, most of them probably sound like common sense—and that's because they are. These are things that make sense. Logically, most of us understand that our time is valuable and want our work to mean something. We all want to be part of an organization that cares about how we're doing and why it is impacting our work ability rather than simply seeing us as a number on a screen that will be replaced if something goes wrong. In principle, everything we just named is reasonable. In practice, the vast majority of those elements are treated as optional or patently unreasonable by higher-ups. It can be time consuming to build a workplace where people are valued for their individuality and the different perspectives and strengths they bring to the table, much less one where that diversity is coveted and actively supported and promoted. The typical workplace doesn't offer many of those fundamental elements at all, eschewing them in favor of results. But as we've already learned and will explore quite a bit going forward, the results that traditional workplace perspectives encourage are rarely optimal and typically leave much room for improvement.

You might be looking at the preceding information and shaking your head. I know it's a lot to take in. I'm not saying that you should be able to create the perfect environment—perfection is never obtainable. I'm pointing out that creating a great workplace might seem like a mystery, but it's actually quite straightforward. What is a great workplace? One where people are appreciated and celebrated. It's a workplace that emphasizes the individual workers as well as how they come together and drive innovation and excellence as a team. None of this is new information, nor is it full of unexpected revelations. Even if you can't implement every single fundamental element into your workplace, there are things you can do to improve your organization and enhance the experience of your workforce.

Let's look at some of the principles that can help you shift the emphasis from the bottom line to the people helping your organization improve.

1. Embrace Individuality: One of the most important things you can do to promote a healthy workplace is to allow people to be themselves. Don't limit yourself to traditional diversity categories such as race, gender, ethnicity, or age. Although attempting to include a variety of these demographics in your workplace is a great idea, hitting quotas is not the best way to promote true diversity and individualism. Instead, look at individuals with different experiences, different perspectives, different ways of thinking, and different core assumptions. You can have a workforce full of employees of all ages, ethnicities, and races, but if they all have the same ideas, perspectives, and worldviews, you aren't going to reap the benefits of a truly diverse team. And it is easier than you might expect to end up in a situation where a group of individuals are "diverse" on paper but not in practice. After all, many of us pursued the same education in search of the same kind of job based on shared beliefs.

Organizations and managers should understand dominant currents in work habits, culture, dress code, governing assumptions, and traditions without accepting them as the "ideal." This is where a more subtle understanding of diversity comes into play. A great organization will transcend the norms in search of individuals whose perspectives and talents can benefit everyone and improve organization prosperity and growth. Think about a creative company—a fashion company, for example—where the workforce norms include flexible hours and rather eclectic styles. You might not expect to see the straitlaced executive focused on data analysis, yet having them in the organization is objectively beneficial when it comes to understanding business trends and making smart market decisions.

A diverse organization that values individuality will enable employees to work in the way that makes them comfortable, appreciate their contribution, and treat their preferences as normal even when they don't fit "industry norms." This also means understanding what biases workers might encounter in the workplace and taking steps to eliminate or overcome them in order to support employees from all walks of life.

2. Share Information: It can be tempting to spin information to suit a specific narrative and hide information that cannot be spun, but the truth is that it is incredibly hard to hide something indefinitely in today's world. Sooner or later, the truth will be revealed. If you've gone out of your way to deceive your employees, they will remember that action and will learn to distrust your words in the future. This, as you might expect, leads only to a fractured work environment where the workforce is constantly second-guessing management, especially if the information in question directly impacts its well-being. Avoid this struggle altogether and simply give your workers the unspun truth yourself before they learn it elsewhere. Taking this approach can only help align the organization and keep everyone on the same page. When employees share the same knowledge, they are more likely to be able to understand different motivations and will compromise in order to produce quality work or create new ideas that are beneficial to everyone involved.

This can be a difficult guideline to follow. There is a myriad of different approaches to information dissemination, and just about everyone has strong feelings as to why their method is the best. Some managers, for example, believe that they should focus primarily on avoiding worrying the staff with information that might not prove to be important. The unfortunate consequence of this perspective, despite its seemingly benign and even praiseworthy intentions, is that if the information proves to be quite important, it will have already begun to impact workers by the time they learn of it. This is often true in cases where an impending change in office processes or norms is being discussed but has not yet been decided upon. By the time the decision has been made to implement changes, it's likely that the majority of the higher-ups in the organization in question have already begun to treat employees and their work as though those changes are already in place. This will naturally lead to confusion and pushback from a workforce that feels as though the changes are sudden and unexpected. The same is true of the manager who wants to avoid bearing bad news. No one wants to break unfortunate information to their coworkers, but refusing to do so crushes the flow of vital information. Even bad news can be mitigated if it is discussed openly and the opportunity to change things is presented.

The idea that information should be honestly conveyed to the workforce is often known as "radical honesty," and it can be difficult to embrace. Opening the communication channels required to implement such a policy can be overwhelming all on its own, and that's before training everyone as to how to use it. Additionally, some information simply can't be shared with everyone. Trade secrets, for example, must remain confidential. And being honest won't necessarily avoid all backlash. The takeaway here is that when you're honest, at least the workforce has the same information, and everyone can work toward a shared vision based on it.

3. Emphasize Strengths: Today's market is an increasingly competitive one in almost every field imaginable, with innovative companies sprouting across the globe. It is more important than ever to create a workforce filled with talented individuals who aren't afraid to take risks and push for innovative solutions to problems old and new alike. On the surface, it might seem like this competition is a good thing for employers. After all, if there is an abundance of talent vying for positions in a specific industry, then losing someone must not be that detrimental. You can always replace them, right? Except that doing this doesn't create a unified workforce. In fact, it doesn't even encourage current employees to put much effort or care into their work. If you view people as disposable, you're likely going to receive disposable work in return.

Focus on hiring great talent and training them to magnify their strengths instead of replacing them. Don't treat your workforce as a disposable entity but as an investment. Work with your employees to identify and enhance their abilities so that they can give you the very best work possible. This improves their effectiveness and productivity, not to mention the loyalty with which they view the organization. And maximizing employees' potential is a great way to create a long-term workforce filled with capable, experienced individuals who are comfortable working together and making innovative or creative suggestions.

Some may find this suggestion to be unreasonable. Investing in employees might seem more costly than replacing them with more experienced talent, at least in the short term. But in the long term you are creating valuable employees with a varied set of skills that allows them to tackle many different situations. Create your own elite workforce instead of hiring them from the outside. You will build a loyal workforce excited to do well and improve your organization. A great employer understands that individuals are valuable. In turn, this will make your organization valuable.

4. Live the Brand: Having a mission statement is important when it comes to building a unified workforce. But it is equally important to understand the difference between shoving an idea down employees' throats and creating something around which they can organically rally. This might sound like an odd thing to say. After all, if you have a good mission statement, shouldn't that be enough to motivate employees?

The idea behind this tip is that you should create a work culture that focuses more on maintaining and forging powerful connections between your organizational values and your personal values—and, by extension, your employees' personal values—than on repeating your mission statement over and over again. It's important to embody that mission statement and to create tangible examples of it throughout the workplace. This enables employees to connect your organization's values with more than lip service. When they see how the company and their coworkers interact with those values on a practical level, they are much more likely to connect the ideas in question with their own values. And when that happens, it becomes even easier to forge a unified workspace founded on shared values and individuality alike. Give your employees the opportunity to internalize company values and interpret those meanings on their own.

For this particular guideline to work, your business must forge your values, not the other way around. It's one thing to create a mission statement that sounds good; it's another to illustrate those values to both your employees and your customers. When workers feel as though your organization's practices embody its purported values, they begin to become more aligned with your goals as well as with their fellow employees. At the same time, this clear demonstration of values in action also enables them to consider what those values mean to them and how they will uphold them in their daily lives.

5. Ensure That the Work Makes Sense: Understanding what your employees are doing and the tasks they are expected to perform is important. I mean this on a more personal level than simply recognizing that one department does a specific set of tasks and another focuses on a different set of tasks. I mean that you should understand what every employee is doing relative to their job title and their strengths. This can be a formidable process in larger companies, but I believe that it is fully worth the time it takes to conduct job reviews and assessments. The idea is that when your employees identify with their work and understand how it fits into the big picture, they are more likely to feel as though their time at work is productive and useful. Match your employees to the work they want to do—the work for which they were hired. There are a few different ways to do this. You can set up more specific job descriptions that are explicit about the tasks expected and required, or you can dramatically loosen those descriptions and allow employees their pick of certain projects or responsibilities (usually in conjunction with fixed job tasks). Either way, enabling workers to do the work they feel passionate about is a fantastic way to create a work environment that exceeds their expectations.

You can't accurately consider productivity in the office without factoring in the underlying fundamental physical issues that might restrict us from working at our best. This includes proper office space and temperature control. Even though it should go without saying, workers need enough space to get their work done effectively and productively. And the temperature in the office must be at a reasonable level—not too hot, not too cold, but just right. If any of these factors are missing, productivity is restricted on a fundamental level.

Proper leadership and management are also important. Nothing is perfect, of course, but you must be confident that you have the right people in the right jobs. If your employees are dissatisfied and unhappy with management, none of the tools I provide in this book will get you anywhere. Leadership and management are critical. Highlighting this, Mavenlink's "Future of Work" survey questioned 1,002 full-time employees in a US corporate environment during September 2019. Forty-five percent of all respondents selected "poor management/leadership" as the top productivity killer.

Culture in a Box

Culture is the fabric of your organization. Whether you like it or not, you have a culture. If it's not spelled out or if you haven't intentionally shaped it, it will drive itself. The problem with its driving itself is that you don't know where you're going; therefore, when you get there, you don't know where you are. This section speaks to a defined culture. It's a *culture in a box* as I like to call it.

What was the best company you ever worked for? It's likely to be the one where you were most productive. Consider what made it so great. Was it great pay, benefits, and a short commute? Most people might think so. But surprisingly, these are not the most important factors. Instead, you likely had a series of challenging duties in an environment where people respected you and challenged you to do your best. You pushed for creative solutions because everyone supported that kind of problem solving. With that in mind, I'm going to explore some principles that make ventures successful and can be applied to organizations of any size.

Why are these important? Well, I doubt that I would have left to start my own firm if my former employer had a strong culture that matched the eloquent words of the mission statement on the wall. In the company's actual measures of excellence (money), I was successful. The work came easy for me, and I was promoted regularly. I led the company in sales and revenue. But it wasn't enough. The company's culture didn't match the lofty statements they professed to follow.

I left that firm because the words on the plaque were never taken seriously. When I packed my belongings in a box, I left with my personal effects and a belief that the way I approached my job, my customers, and my life was

more effective than the corporate culture I was leaving behind. This box held my own culture: my *culture in a box*.

Culture in a box represents the way we will build our companies, with a focus on all of the people involved. You won't find a mission statement on the wall. There is no need for one. When your actions match your core values for living, you'll find that amazing things can happen. You will increase your revenue, reduce your turnover, increase your customer retention, and get rave reviews when people ask for references from your customers. Even better, you'll get rave reviews from those employees that you let go.

The following are the concepts of a culture in a box. Applying these principles should improve your profits, your life, your health, and those of your company and employees.

1. Customers Second: Every *second* fiber of our company should be directed toward the customer. The first is to the employees. Employees are your most valuable assets, not customers. Customers come and go, but when treated properly, employees are there to stay. If your employees are happy, they will do better work, be healthier, and serve customers better. Employees first, customers second, and money third. If you follow those tenets, the money always comes.

2. Work Is Life: Don't separate work from life. Life consists of 24-hour segments. All of it is life, not just the nonworking hours. In fact, work composes more than 50 percent of your waking life. By including work as a part of life, employees become more responsible.

3. Respect the Corporate Documents: A corporation is nothing more than a piece of paper filed with the secretary of state. It's easy to obtain, yet it carries tremendous weight. This document represents a means to improve our lives. That's why the concept of improving our lives should be a basic tenet of the values of any company. The corporation exists so we can all learn and grow.

4. No Titles: We do not have titles in our company unless we travel to Asia, and even then we only implement them only because it can affect how well we do business there. Every employee in the company is critical to the success of the organization, from the person who makes the sale to the custodian who cleans the restroom. Imagine how unproductive the office would be with filthy restrooms. Every job is important for the enterprise. If it is not, then the job should not exist.

5. Embrace Dynamic Hierarchy: The CEO must set the tone of the culture and understand when to change the direction of the company or offer new products and services. The CEO must "report and be reported to." If we take the metaphor of a floor full of glass offices—the ideal environment—the CEO would be sitting in the middle, with all the departments working around him or her so everyone's actions were transparent. But in order to learn, the CEO must also look up, not always down.

6. Liberal Vacation Policy: We had a tacit unlimited vacation policy. It was not published or publicized, but there was flexibility when one needed to take time off. Yet, the concept of "no vacation policy" generally does not work. It leads to a false feeling of freedom and often backfires. For example, I've seen employees not take vacation because they simply did not want to do so. I've had to force employees to take vacations in some instances. It's healthy and productive for employees to take extended breaks. It's important for mental health and for increased engagement in the firm when they return. On the other hand, in some of these firms where they promote an "unlimited vacation policy," it's dishonest. Employees feel that the pressure to continually work is so great in these firms that when they do go on vacation, they often feel that they won't have a job when they return. There is one firm that comes to mind whose culture was, "If you don't work on Saturdays, don't bother to come in on Sundays." Awful.

7. Design Warm Office Spaces: Get out of the cookie-cutter cubicles and rectangular office spaces. Design a creative atmosphere where employees can enjoy their surroundings. Work and life must be made to coexist and become almost seamless. In our firm, we created an atmosphere that is akin to someone's home. When walking into our lobby, it could very well be a living room.

8. Train and Promote from Within: Hire smart, train well, and promote from within. Outsiders who come with 10 or 20 years of experience are less likely to fit in with your culture. This is not a rule, however, and sometimes it is necessary to infuse the company with a key hire if you're certain that they fit into the culture and have skills you need.

9. Zero Tolerance for Office Politics: Jockeying for positions, denigrating others, talking behind people's back about their work or personal choices. There should be tolerance for mistakes and differences of opinion. However, office politics should be treated with contempt and disdain—no compromises and zero tolerance. Office politics are cancerous and, unless discovered and destroyed quickly, they will spread and annihilate your company. As a strong leader, you must be aware of any office politics by staying close to your employees.

10. Reinvent Your Company: Look to reinvent your company constantly. If there is one aspect of life you can count on, it is change. The world has never been a more rapidly changing environment and it's changing faster and faster all the time. The speed of business is likely to increase along with technology and global reach. Look at each change as an opportunity to create new products and services to meet the changing environment.

The preceding principles work. Customers will get the service they enjoy and that they rarely get from other firms. Be the only firm in your industry that operates in this fashion and brand this culture heavily. A strong company culture will create the stability that will improve the lives of everyone in your company. We focused our energy on issues important to our customers and families, on redefining the model to get a better solution, and on living the values set forth earlier. I can do that with confidence because I know that is how we actually work and live.

In the end, all of this translates into good business. Employees who are happy are better at their jobs. And if they're better at their jobs, they beat the competition and the company wins—and the money always follows. So tell me what you remember about that great company you worked for.

The Five Buckets of Productivity

Each of the following five buckets represent the opportunity to improve your firm. In many cases, your firm is already performing well in some buckets; in others, there is work to be done. Each of these has a process that will take time to engage and employ. Begin each in one department or division of the company as a beta and expand from there.

The following chapters will address each of these buckets in detail. As you read through them, you'll determine whether you want to make the associated changes in your own company. The goal is to get 30 hours out of every day. By the end of this book, you'll see how that's possible and how much additional revenue your employees will generate for the company.

About Remote Work

When it comes to productivity, many CEOs believe that everyone must be working in the same room at the same time to do well. And while the principle sounds like a solid one—people working together are more productive than those working alone—it's not necessarily an accurate one. In fact, there

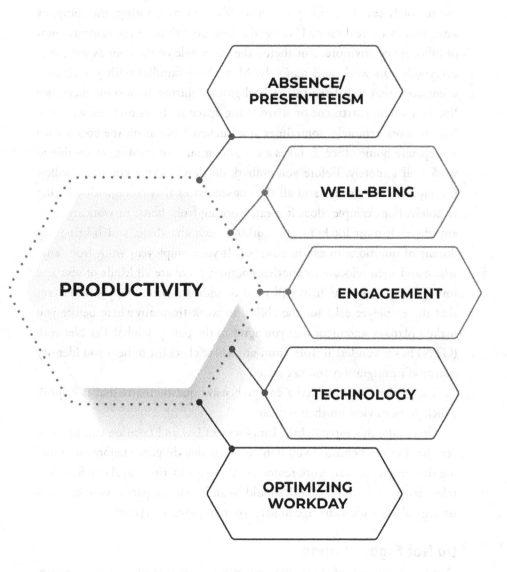

ABSENCE/
PRESENTEEISM

WELL-BEING

PRODUCTIVITY

ENGAGEMENT

TECHNOLOGY

OPTIMIZING
WORKDAY

is evidence that working outside the office, be it from home or elsewhere, can actually boost productivity by quite a bit. The 2020 pandemic teaches us a lot about remote work productivity. There's no question that working remotely can be highly productive. With no commuting, the company saves money on real estate because the firm doesn't need the same amount of office space anymore. But there's the other side of the coin as well. Not everybody can work well remotely. Many have families with young children; dogs that will bark in the background during important meetings; live in a small apartment or share living space with roommates who also have to work remotely, sometimes at a kitchen table or on the couch with no separate home office. It takes a certain amount of training to be able to work well remotely. Before you embark on developing a company policy, it's important to understand all the consequences that come with working remotely. For example, does it mean working from home or working from anywhere? It most likely means working from anywhere, which brings up dozens of questions to ask in advance. If your employees work from anywhere and then relocate to another country, there are all kinds of visa and immigration issues the firm will need to address. Therefore, it's important that the employee asks for the ability to work from anywhere before you make a blanket statement that you agree to the policy. Global Tax Network (GTN) has a wonderful work-from-anywhere checklist to help you identify potential immigration and tax issues.[*]

The Littler Law Firm has a comprehensive questionnaire that is helpful, which you can view on their website.

Don't take this topic lightly. Employment law and taxation can bite you very hard in the behind if you don't do your due diligence before announcing that employees can work remotely. After considering the above first, let's take a look at why remote work should be an important part of your business strategy along with some tips to keep your employees engaged.

Do Not Fight Change

One major outcome of the 2020 pandemic is a veritable revolution in the way the business industry operates. Many organizations simply weren't ready and

---

[*]   Global Tax Network US, L., 2020. *Work Anywhere Checklist For Your Mobility Program.* [online] Info.gtn.com. Available at: <https://info.gtn.com/work-anywhere-checklist-for-your -mobility-program>.

able to adapt to the changes that COVID-19 wrought in the workplace. This is understandable to a certain extent. After all, who would have predicted that the world would change so dramatically and so quickly into one where working from home was mandatory?

However, it's important to take the time now to recognize the difficulties your business faced as the demand to be flexible and to adapt your business operations around an immovable barrier increased. For many, one of the major takeaways from the surge in work-at-home positions will be that their infrastructure is nowhere near modern and mobile enough to respond to sudden change.

Many business owners and CEOs might be reading this and assuming that the pandemic was a once-in-a-lifetime issue and that once it fades, they won't have to worry about supporting working from home on any significant level. This is a poor take for many reasons. As we'll discuss, remote work is actually a great tool for job satisfaction, retention, and engagement. Beyond that, however, the refusal to adapt to today's societal trends is a surefire way to fail.

The pandemic might have been unforeseen, but that doesn't mean that the light it is shining upon remote work and digital workplaces is less valid. Industry acceptance of remote work positions has been increasing for years, and it is unlikely that will change anytime soon. The best course of action is to take a hard look at your recovery plans and how they function in reality. This is a great time to assess your goals as a business and how your organization and interpretation of modern business operations impacts your ability to sink or swim.

Radical change might not be easy, but as COVID-19 has illustrated, it is a necessity for many to keep their business healthy and their employees engaged and productive.

Working from Home Boosts Job Satisfaction and Employee Retention

While remote work might have become the norm almost overnight, it's important to take a look at how that change has impacted employees and their views about their position and how they work on a daily basis. One survey of company managers found that 78 percent of respondents stated that offering telecommuting and flexible schedules for the foreseeable future is one of their most effective options to boost employee retention that doesn't involve increased monetary compensation.[*]

Supporting these findings is a global workplace study of more than 15,000 individuals located in more than 100 nations across the world. The research found that 80 percent of respondents would opt for a position with flexible scheduling and remote work options over one without when deciding between multiple employment offers.[†] That same study found that 32 percent of respondents believed that regular remote work options would improve their satisfaction more than a higher role in the organization.

Further underlining the importance of flexible work options, a Gallup poll found that 54 percent of the office workers surveyed would quit their job in favor of another that offered remote work opportunities.[‡] And, perhaps even more interesting, one study found that two-thirds of the respondents said they would quit their job if their newfound flexible working options were revoked.[§] Yet another study found that employees who work from home tend to put in more hours but feel better about their jobs despite it.[¶]

Employee Engagement

Having an engaged employee is vital to productivity. Workers who are present but not engaged accomplish relatively little, and what they do manage to finish is generally poorer in quality than that of employees who are actively engaged with their work. With this in mind, according to the same Gallup poll previously referenced, it's important to note that remote working, even if not every day, has been shown to significantly increase engagement among employees.[**]

---

[*]   Crain's New York Business. 2019. Work-Life Integration: The Customized Approach. [online] Available at: <https://www.crainsnewyork.com/sponsored-future-work/work-life-integration-customized-approach>.

[†]   Iwgplc.com. 2020. IWG Global Workspace Survey - Flexible Working - IWG Plc. [online] Available at: <https://www.iwgplc.com/global-workspace-survey-2019>.

[‡]   Hickman, A. and Robison, J., 2020. Is Working Remotely Effective? Gallup Research Says Yes. [online] Gallup.com. Available at: <https://www.gallup.com/workplace/283985/working-remotely-effective-gallup-research-says-yes.aspx>.

[§]   2019. Workplace Survey Results 2019. [ebook] Available at: <https://marketingassets.staples.com/m/5644f1362b2dfad2/original/Staples-Workplace-Survey-2019.pdf>.

[¶]   Owllabs.com. 2019. 2019 State Of Remote Work Report. [online] Available at: <https://www.owllabs.com/state-of-remote-work/2019>.

[**]   Hickman, A. and Robison, J., 2020. Is Working Remotely Effective? Gallup Research Says Yes. [online] Gallup.com. Available at: <https://www.gallup.com/workplace/283985/working-remotely-effective-gallup-research-says-yes.aspx>.

Employees who work from home are, in general, more likely to pick a time and place to work that suits their specific needs. For some, that might mean sitting in a completely silent room and focusing on nothing but their keyboard, a scenario rarely present in today's bustling workplaces. Others might find that a room with inspiring décor is the best option to truly raise their morale. Whatever their choice, remote workers are more likely to give themselves the surroundings and circumstances most conducive to their engagement and success than they would if they were working from a physical office.

Productivity Boost

Working remotely is a great way to boost employee productivity. And that's the goal at the end of the day, right? It was previously assumed that working from home might mean that remote workers would face more distractions than their in-office counterparts, but current research says that's not the case.

One survey found that employees working from home were 20 to 25 percent more productive than their coworkers working in the office.[*] Another found that 75 percent of respondents said they worked from home specifically because there were fewer distractions, enabling them to truly focus on their work.[†] In fact, research as far back as 2012 showed that remote work might very well be the key to optimal worker productivity.[‡]

Productivity and Engagement Tips

Finally, let's take a look at how you can best engage remote workers, utilize all the benefits that working from home gives them, and channel that into increased productivity. The first thing to keep in mind is that while the location of work might have changed, the need for individual attention has not. Reach out to your employees and find out what their work environment is like at home as well as the challenges they might be facing. Understanding

---

[*] Wilkie, D., 2019. Why Are Companies Ending Remote Work?. [online] SHRM. Available at: <https://www.shrm.org/resourcesandtools/hr-topics/employee-relations/pages/drawbacks-to-working-at-home-.aspx?utm_source=link_wwwv9&utm_campaign=item_288956&utm_medium=copy>.

[†] Simovic, D., 2019. The Ultimate List of Remote Work *Statistics—2020* Edition. [online] SmallBizGenius. Available at: <https://www.smallbizgenius.net/by-the-numbers/remote-work-statistics/#gref>.

[‡] O'Toole, K., 2012. Researchers: Flexibility May Be the Key to Increased Productivity. [online] Stanford Graduate School of Business. Available at: <https://www.gsb.stanford.edu/insights/researchers-flexibility-may-be-key-increased-productivity>.

their situation is a good way to adapt tasks and deadlines to play to their strengths.*

Another tip to boost employee engagement while working remotely is to host a webinar or send out detailed instructions about how to use video equipment and other online work tools. Do this even for things that seem obvious. You never know how many employees cope well with technology in the office but have little idea how to access or engage with anything outside that scope.† Again, keep your workers' strengths and potential weaknesses in mind and take action to avoid potential pitfalls. Making their day as smooth and straightforward as possible will ensure that their attention remains fully on their work.

For further reading about productivity, see Appendix A.

---

*   Robison, J., 2020. COVID-19 Has My Teams Working Remotely: A Guide for Leaders. [online] Gallup.com. Available at: <https://www.gallup.com/workplace/288956/covid-teams-working-remotely-guide-leaders.aspx>.

†   Matuson, R., 2020. How Leaders Can Keep Remote Employees Engaged and Productive During Tumultuous Times. [online] Forbes. Available at: <https://www.forbes.com/sites/robertamatuson/2020/03/10/how-leaders-can-keep-remote-employees-engaged-and-productive-during-these-tumultuous-times/#134080b94b1c>.

CHAPTER THREE

Key Component #1— Absence Management and Presenteeism

CEO: Our next step in the company is to address absence from work. I think it's obvious why this is important. If you are not at work, our company cannot produce, market, or sell our products. It's that simple. If someone is out, the firm is losing money. If we're losing money, we can't grow. I think you all know how things snowball from there. I remember when I was a driver at UPS—it was my first job out of college. My manager would say, "Let's get these trucks out of here. If a truck's not moving, we aren't making money." If a driver was absent, that affected his route. It was expensive to replace him, even for a day. I'm referring here to *physical* absence. There is another insidious kind of absence to look out for: presenteeism. This refers to being at work physically but not mentally. You can physically be here but also *not* be here at the same time. Studies show that in some cases, the problem of presenteeism is 10 times worse for a company than absenteeism. It's a real issue, and we can't sweep it under the rug. We're going to spend a lot of our time today talking about that.

Bethany: How do we identify it?

CEO: The first step is to measure it. Does anybody have any ideas about how to do that?

Bethany: Look at what people are doing on their computers?

CEO: That's one way, but I'm against spying on employees. We'll do that only if we suspect theft or fraud. Besides, that won't solve the issue. It'll just put a bandage on it. If someone can't use their computer for nonwork-related matters, they'll use their phone instead.

Mark: Ask people.

CEO: Exactly. Later I'll speak about engagement, because presenteeism is related. We can measure engagement through surveys. We can do the same with presenteeism as long as people are honest. If it's a short survey, I find that most people are honest about not being present.

Years ago—in 2007—the World Health Organization published a survey for employers to use to assess absenteeism and presenteeism. That information is still relevant today. The big takeaway is: *You can't manage what you can't measure.* There is a metric for measuring almost everything, and that includes the current topic. I'm going to break this chapter into two parts: absenteeism and presenteeism. We'll take a look at what each of these means for businesses and how to recognize and address the problem.

The following are examples of the causes of absenteeism and presenteeism:

- Heavy workloads
- Stress
- Lack of appreciation for the work
- Poor managers
- Poor working conditions
- Poor morale
- Substandard compensation and benefits
- Abuse at work, including bullying and harassment

I've seen all of these in various organizations. They can all be fixed when you know the problem.

Absenteeism

When people don't come to work, the cost to an organization is high. I think of this cost as waste, and your employees should as well. After all, everybody loses when someone is out sick. The exception here is planned time off. Holidays and vacations are a win–win. Employees get the rest they need to come back more engaged and more productive than ever. I look at holidays and vacations the same way I look at sleep. We need our sleep to be happy, engaged, healthy, and productive. The same applies to holidays and vacations.

When employees are legitimately sick, it's important to offer them help to get well as soon as possible and bounce right back into work. In this situation, you both win. You get healthy employees who feel well and make it back to work revitalized and grateful for the help. You both feel good. It's another win–win situation. And it's important to think about absenteeism caused by illness in this way, because sick or absent employees are expensive and unproductive. You get hit twice: the expense of paying for someone who is not working and the productivity hit from the employee who is not working and therefore not productive. You might need temporary staff in some cases, as well as time from managers to deal with unexpected absences, train a new person, and handle a significant loss of production and quality control. Your customers suffer, as do coworkers who are put under more stress and become less productive as a result. One study shows that these employees become as much as 29 percent less productive when someone is absent.

I've worked for Fortune 500 companies as well as my own firm, and each business had different ways of dealing with absent employees. With my firm, we had a temporary agency find us a replacement as soon as possible. I did not want to get hit with a loss of productivity and the fallout of other employees taking on the extra burden of a sick or absent employee. You can't always find temps who are skilled labor, of course, but the benefit of finding temporary workers is that they are often very good at what they do. We've converted many temporary workers to permanent employees. I've even created positions in order to hire some of those temporary workers. That's how talented they were. When I worked for one Fortune 500 company, on the other hand, the company policy was "no temporary workers." I was on the executive committee of this firm as one of the five highest-ranking officials in the company and argued with the CFO that such a policy was unproductive. He didn't care. He was myopic and could look only at the cost of a temporary worker versus the loss of productivity in the company. The CEO left those decisions to the CFO, and so the policy remained.

The bottom line? The best way to avoid a drop in your organization's productivity and the financial losses that accompany absenteeism is to help keep your employees as healthy as possible. Offer aid when they're genuinely sick so that they can recover as quickly as possible, minimizing downtime and the potential expense of hiring a temporary worker in their place. But, as always, a good offense is better than a good defense, and maintaining a healthy workplace is the best plan. Sometimes that's just not possible, of course, which leads us to the next section.

But before we get there, one more thought on this topic. I was on the phone recently with the IT help desk to get support regarding my computer. The technician apologized to me that it took so long for him to get to me. He commented that on Friday afternoon, it's funny how many people don't feel well after lunch and say they need to go home. He lost three technicians after lunch. It happens all the time. Then he added that they often "call in sick" when everyone knows they don't want to come to work. We both laughed at this behavior, but it's actually quite telling. These employees who are comfortable lying about their health are not engaged and simply are not good employees. While you cannot let someone go for being ill, you can do so if they are not working to the standards of the company. This is an employment issue, and an employment lawyer should be consulted to determine your rights as an employer. I'm disturbed by how many people feel comfortable lying to their employers and consider sick days any days they feel like they want to take off. I've even seen it portrayed in movies as an acceptable means of behavior. Employers are not stupid. What's happened over time is that employers no longer ask employees if they are actually sick but have changed their policies and are giving employees paid time off (PTO). This solves the ethical problem of trying to determine whether employees are actually telling the truth. Employees are entitled to a certain amount of PTO, making use of it any way they like. The distrust here is unfortunate. It leads to greater issues, which we'll discuss later.

Measuring Absenteeism

Before you can decide what approach to absenteeism is best for your business, you first must know how much of a problem it is at your workplace. You can't accurately fix something when you don't know the extent that it impacts your business. Here are a few steps to follow as you measure absenteeism in your company.

Know Your Absence Rate: Option One

Your HRIS system should have this information at your fingertips. If not, that's an entirely different issue. You'll need to get your arms around the metric. The finance department might use a more complex formula than the following one, but just for reference, here's one from consultant Gijs Houtzagers.

$$ACE = (ML (WH + EBC) + S (RH + SBC) + OC) / E$$

Let's break down some of those factors and variables:

- ACE—Total costs of absenteeism per employee for a defined period

- ML—Total employee hours lost to absenteeism for a defined period, including illness, accidents, compassionate absences (e.g., funeral) and emergencies, but excluding annual leave
- WH—Weighted average hourly pay for the various occupational groups in the organization
- EBC—Cost of employee benefits per hour per employee (= 35 percent of WH)
- S—Supervisor hours lost in dealing with absenteeism for the defined period
- E—Total number of employees
- RH—Average hourly pay for supervisors
- SBC—Costs of supervisor benefits per hour per supervisor (= 35 percent of RH)
- OC—Estimation of other costs
  o Temporary staff
  o Training time for temporary staff
  o Loss of production
  o Quality loss
  o Overtime for replacement of absenteeism
  o Costs of external agencies that provide support on absenteeism
  o Costs of HR dealing with absenteeism

Know Your Absence Rate: Option Two

If option one seems a bit too complex, don't worry. There are easier ways. I found the following measurement tool from Rachel Blakey-Grey in her article for *Patriot** to be very useful. Let's go through a sample problem so that you can more easily visualize how the equation works.

1. First, find the average number of employees. At the beginning of the month, you had seven employees. At the end of the month, you had nine. Your average number of employees is eight ([9 + 7]/2).

---

*   Blakely-Gray, R., 2018. Absenteeism Rate | How to Calculate & Use Absence Rate In Business. [online] Patriot Software. Available at: <https://www.patriotsoftware.com/blog/payroll/how-to-calculate-absenteeism-rate/>.

2. Second, calculate your total workdays in the period. Your business is open Monday through Friday. There were no holidays in October. Your total number of workdays is 23.
3. Third, find the number of workdays lost to absenteeism. Workdays are eight hours long in your business. One employee missed one day and another employee missed one day. In total, your employees were absent for two full days. Another employee was gone for an additional 4 hours. First, divide the 4-hour day by eight hours to get 0.5. Then, add 0.5 and 2 to get a total of 2.5 missed days.
4. Finally, plug your numbers into the absenteeism rate formula:

   Absenteeism rate = (8 x 2.5)/(8 x 23)

   Absenteeism rate = 20/184

   Absenteeism rate = 0.11

To turn your absenteeism rate into a percentage, multiply it by 100. Your absenteeism rate during that month was approximately 11 percent.

What Do These Numbers Mean?

The Bureau of Labor Statistics estimates that the average absentee rate is 2.9 percent. This is a good statistic to start with when looking at your own numbers, but every industry is different. Your culture plays a part, too. The point to keep in mind is that absenteeism reduces productivity no matter what the number is. And though solutions are more important than statistics here, you won't know if the solutions work unless you have the starting point of your absenteeism rate to use as a comparison as potential solutions are implemented. I have not found a better means than this to determine if a company's absenteeism rate actually decreases.

Why does finding a solution matter? Because the net results impact your company. According to workforce solution company Circadian, unscheduled absenteeism costs roughly $3,600 per year for each hourly worker and $2,650 each year for salaried employees. Even a 1 percent or half a percent decrease in absenteeism can reduce those costs.

Presenteeism

You know more about absenteeism now, but what about presenteeism? It might seem odd to imply that employees who aren't missing work are a problem, but a growing body of research, including a recent Global Corporate Challenge (GCC) study, finds that presenteeism can cause ten times more financial loss for businesses than absenteeism. That's largely because presenteeism is more insidious than absenteeism. Whereas it's possible to measure absenteeism, for example, using one of the previously cited tactics, it's far more difficult to determine the prevalence of presenteeism in the workplace because the employees experiencing it are physically present. They are in their offices, sitting behind their desks, and seemingly working on their daily tasks. To the outside observer, most of them probably look busy and productive. In reality, however, many of them are not working or not working to their full potential. And when employees don't work to their full potential, they're costing the business money.

What Is Presenteeism?

Defining presenteeism can be almost as difficult as understanding how to measure it. At its most basic, the term refers to being present but not fully engaged with work. And while that might seem like a fairly straightforward and broad definition, it's the nuance that makes the concept a bit harder to accurately define. When you think about employees who are at work but not engaged, for example, your thoughts might drift to someone intentionally checking out of their tasks and spending time chatting with coworkers or browsing the Internet instead of focusing on their work. This is not the situation described by the term "presenteeism," however, as those issues are fairly simple to recognize. Instead, the word refers to a much more subtle problem: employees who are at work but are unable to focus and fully engage with their tasks despite doing their best.

Presenteeism can be hard to detect because the workers in question generally appear to be working hard and they are likely doing the best they can given their circumstances. The main problem is that they struggle with some kind of health issue that limits their ability to engage with the workplace. You might be surprised at the impact that seemingly small problems can have on productivity. It's important to understand that the issues your employees struggle with don't have to be something huge such as cancer or heart disease. In fact, presenteeism is insidious particularly because it thrives on unseen issues that impact how people feel but not necessarily how they look or behave when interacting with coworkers. Someone with particularly severe allergies, for example, might look fine but have symptoms that impact their overall well-being, including persistent headaches and "mental fog." One study published in the *Journal of Occupational and Environmental Medicine* found that employees with chronic allergies and allergic conditions impacted worker productivity by 10 percent[*]. More recent research collated and analyzed by the American Academy of Allergy, Asthma, and Immunology found that workers with allergic rhinitis rarely missed work (2.3 percent of respondents) but experienced a 32.5 percent impairment while in the workplace.[†] In other words, they were present but unable to function as well as they should.

This is the crux of the problem with presenteeism. Employees might be struggling with something most of us perceive as fairly benign, something that rarely causes trouble severe enough to miss work. But they experience significant performance loss despite showing up and attempting to meet their deadlines and complete their tasks. The problem isn't with employee determination or intention but rather with their ability to engage with the workplace. And that is something that is more difficult to recognize and measure than the obvious productivity loss from an employee who spends their time wandering around the office and chatting rather than sitting at their desk and working. Employees can be bored, play games on their computers, shop on Amazon, read a book on Kindle, or a dozen other activities that essentially are not productive for the business. You'll read this many times, but lack of engagement is a major culprit of the cause and loss of productivity. Poor management is another—managers need to be trained in Compassionate Productivity. The best managers are those who have employees that want to do well to help the manager succeed.

What Causes Presenteeism?

Another problem presented by presenteeism is determining its origin. It's much easier to understand the reasons why people are absent from the

---

[*]   Burton, W., Conti, D., Chen, C., Schultz, A. and Edington, D., 2001. The Impact of Allergies and Allergy Treatment on Worker Productivity. *Journal of Occupational and Environmental Medicine*, 43(1): 64–71.

[†]   The American Academy of Allergy, Asthma & Immunology. 2017. The Impact of Allergic Rhinitis on Work Productivity | AAAAI. [online] Available at: <https://www.aaaai.org/global /latest-research-summaries/New-Research-from-JACI-In-Practice/allergic-rhinitis-work>.

workplace. Most of them are ill, injured, or on vacation. Understanding this enables company leaders to plan and implement effective policies and programs designed to reduce absenteeism in general. With presenteeism, however, finding the root cause of the problem can be just as difficult as locating the culprits. Are the employees in question unhappy with their work? Are they worried about personal issues that are impacting their time spent working? There are many potential causes, and each one might require a different approach to resolve it.

There is one big factor that many employees who experience presenteeism report: stress. According to the International Foundation of Employee Benefit Plans,* workplace stress can significantly impact employees and employers in a number of different ways. With employees, it can result not only in presenteeism but also in physical and mental health issues. This, in turn, can lead to increased absenteeism. That's a big problem when, according to the same study, presenteeism alone costs businesses $150 billion a year in lost productivity. Combine that with the losses resulting from absenteeism, and it's easy to see how dangerous these issues can be to your business. And if your presenteeism rate is 10 times that of your absenteeism rate, you can see where the real problem lies. The questions are how to isolate incidents of presenteeism and what to do about them.

Measuring Presenteeism

It's more difficult to measure presenteeism, but it's not impossible. The most effective method is to conduct surveys. You can use the survey to determine how your employees are feeling while working, how much time they're spending actively engaged with their work, and what might be influencing their feelings. When you have this information, it becomes easier to design a solution. As a manager, I asked that all my direct reports come to me with a problem as well as a solution. I wanted employees to learn how to think through problems themselves. And when they came with a solution, they would feel empowered and engaged, two feelings that enhance a person's ability to function and be more productive while living to the fullest.

---

* n.d. *Stress in the Workplace: Meeting the Challenge.* [ebook] healthadvocate.com. Available at: <http://healthadvocate.com/downloads/webinars/stress-workplace.pdf>.

In addition to the preceding methods, there are some more specific ones that can make measuring presenteeism less of a mystery. Here are some detailed solutions that might be a good fit for your workplace.

Presenteeism Scoring

One of the most effective and well-established presenteeism measuring options is the Health and Work Performance questionnaire developed by the World Health Organization.[*] Working to measure both presenteeism and absenteeism, the survey looks at employee health on a wide scale, asking workers to discuss how they'd rate their physical and mental health overall. The questionnaire also looks at more specific issues that can impact workplace productivity such as arthritis, migraines, chronic back pain, high blood pressure, ulcers, and diabetes while also asking employees if they have received effective treatment for the issues in question. Because it casts such a wide net and collects an array of information, the Health and Work Performance questionnaire is a great way to gauge the overall health of your workforce quickly and fairly easily. Honest answers from employees are essential in surveys such as this one. Emphasizing that their responses will not impact their job security is one way to help encourage employees to be truthful about any health conditions they might be facing.

Employee Satisfaction Surveys

Employee satisfaction surveys are designed to gauge worker happiness and engagement in the workplace. This might not immediately seem like a great option to explore presenteeism in particular, however these questionnaires are a fantastic supplement to other measuring solutions. Understanding whether your employees are happy is an important step in identifying potential issues, especially when paired with surveys that also ask for information about their overall health—both mental and physical—and the type of struggles they face every day while working. These responses can often reveal small health issues that not even the respondents recognize as problems having the potential to impact productivity and happiness at work.

---

[*]   Hcp.med.harvard.edu. n.d. The World Health Organization Health and Work Performance Questionnaire (HPQ). [online] Available at: <https://www.hcp.med.harvard.edu/hpq/info.php>.

Health and Wellness Numbers

With issues such as presenteeism, the more information you have available, the better equipped you will be to establish the programs and policies necessary to help minimize the problem as much as possible. One great way to keep an eye on any potential issues is to keep tabs on your overall health and wellness numbers. You can do this a few different ways. First, your benefits and insurance partners should be able to supply you with reports and data to paint an overview of how healthy your workforce is in general. Next, pair those reports with observations and input from your managers. They are on the front lines and are often the best equipped to recognize health problems that employees either don't report or issues where they don't receive proper treatment. What do your managers see as symptoms and signs of any team challenges related to health issues, and what kind of intervention is available to them to help encourage the affected employees to seek treatment? Routine discussions with your managers can help provide an invaluable supplement to the information you receive from your partners as well as your employees themselves if you use additional health surveys to measure presenteeism.

Client Satisfaction

Another smart way to measure presenteeism is to look at client satisfaction—with a few caveats. If your clients are happy and receiving the information and help they need when they need it, your employees are likely productive and well engaged. The opposite is also true. If your clients are not receiving the assistance they need, your employees might very well be poorly engaged and unproductive. In this way, it can be possible to gauge presenteeism via client satisfaction alone. With that said, however, it is important to avoid placing too much emphasis on this form of measurement, because it can be difficult to know exactly what causes employee excellence or failure in this area. Sick employees with close professional relationships with clients might push themselves to provide as much assistance as possible even when ill; employees who are overworked might be shirking their share of the responsibility, leaving unsatisfied clients in their wake. It is not as simple as "happy clients = happy employees." Placing too much stock in this correlation alone will not provide the accurate measure of presenteeism you must have to develop effective solutions to combat the problem.

Clear Goals and Self-Assessments

Because presenteeism is so difficult to identify on the "front lines," it is often easier to first identify a drop in productivity and then explore the reason behind it. This method is only as effective as your efforts to regularly track employees' productivity and progress in the form of both self-assessments and managerial observation. Explore both data sets frequently and watch for any unexpected dips in productivity or the quality of an employee's work. When you notice a persistent issue, speak with the employee in question and determine what might be happening that could cause their performance to drop. Whether they're struggling with a health issue or a personal problem at home, or they are burned out or overworked, the best way to address potentially damaging issues is to meet them head-on. After you know who is struggling and why, you can begin to determine how best to fix the problem and better enable your workforce to optimize their efforts.

The best way to minimize presenteeism and absenteeism is to stay on top of your employees' health and wellness needs. Build a corporate culture that promotes the idea that physical and mental health are top priorities and consider offering remote work options so that employees can stay home when ill and still contribute to the office. Chances are good that they will be more productive from the comfort of their home than they would be in the office when they're not feeling their best. When you create an environment in which employees feel comfortable putting their health first, you'll reap the benefits of a healthy and happy workforce dedicated to the company and willing to expend time and effort on their needs.

Don't be discouraged by the relatively difficult nature of tracking presenteeism and absenteeism. It can be hard, but it's not impossible. When you have the groundwork in place, maintaining an up-to-date body of data will be an easy ongoing process that doesn't require much in the way of time or resources. And if you're interested in learning more about employee well-being and how it can impact not only your workforce's performance but also your own, the next chapter offers plenty of details to help you get started.

These kinds of solutions can help mitigate the task of addressing presenteeism and minimizing its impact on your business.

Addressing Presenteeism

Recognizing and measuring presenteeism is important, but understanding how to minimize the problem and offer employees the best chance possible to optimize their productivity and engagement is equally so. There are a few different tactics to use to address presenteeism and boosting workplace morale and ability on a long-term basis. Let's take a look at a few options that can help you give your workforce the tools it needs to perform as best as it possibly can.

Clear Communication About Leave Options

Whereas keeping employees in the office might seem like the best option, it should be fairly clear given the information we've discussed throughout this chapter that this is not always the case. In fact, sometimes offering employees alternative work options can help significantly boost their engagement and productivity. One of the best things you can do to reduce presenteeism is to ensure that your employees know what kind of leave options are available to them. This includes vacation days and sick days, of course, but also things such as FMLA leave and company-specific leave solutions available when employees are unwell or otherwise struggling with a health issue. Remote work is a good balance between forcing employees to come to work when they aren't feeling well and losing their presence entirely due to sick days. Working from home can help keep sick employees engaged with the workplace while still caring for their health and recovering from whatever is ailing them. This might not be a permanent solution for chronic issues, but it can have a significant impact for short-term problems.

Reexamine Organizational Culture

We've already discussed how important it is to foster a work environment that values employees as individuals, including their health and well-being. So to many, this potential solution might not be surprising. One way to reduce presenteeism is to create an organizational culture that values worker health and emphasizes the importance of staying home or utilizing remote working options when employees are unwell. This step is important, because offering leave options and flexible working solutions might seem effective on paper but might not be as impactful as hoped for if your organizational culture inadvertently encourages employees to work in the office regardless of the health issues they are facing. Make sure that your corporate culture supports healthy employees and that your managers understand the importance of allowing employees the space they need to make the right work choices for their health. This includes working from home or taking sick days rather than powering through their symptoms and struggling to get through the day.

Look at Employee Wellness Initiatives

One particularly effective strategy to target and minimize presenteeism is the introduction of employee wellness initiatives in the workplace. These programs seek to take proactive steps to address various kinds of health issues before they become a serious problem. The human resources department will generally drive this. It's important that these wellness programs are structured properly, otherwise they will be a complete waste of money. At the very basic level, a wellness program will provide employees with pamphlets and other communication materials on how to improve their health. One month may be on smoking cessation, another month on exercise, and so forth. Very sophisticated wellness programs will offer to give you free a blood test to preempt any diseases or conditions that may otherwise go untreated and then have a greater detrimental effect on your health. Some provide gym memberships and even massages. The idea is that if your employees have an easy way to address certain health issues, the workforce in general will likely experience fewer illnesses in general. This kind of program also helps encourage an organizational culture that values wellness and encourages employees to pay attention to their health and take action when they aren't feeling as well as they should. Establishing employee wellness initiatives can also encourage employees who have been struggling with health issues to seek treatment or, at the very least, receive a diagnosis or examination that grants them more insight into the problem and how they can treat it. When employees have easy and affordable options to help boost their overall health, everyone benefits.

Offer Health Benefits

Along the same line as the option previously described, offering health benefits can significantly improve your workforce health and productivity. I'm not talking only about health insurance here. I'm also including things such as free or discounted gym memberships and nutritional consultations along with on-site fitness solutions and free vaccinations. Encouraging your employees to stay as healthy as possible and offering them easy and affordable ways to do so is a great way to minimize both absenteeism and presenteeism. Anything you can reasonably do to make it simple for your employees to improve and maintain their health is something to consider implementing in your workplace.

Find the Right Balance

Finally, take some time to find the right balance between promoting employee health and returning workers on-site as quickly as possible. It can be difficult to encourage employees to stay home when sick while still expecting them to return as quickly as possible, but striking that balance is an important step in reducing presenteeism. Some of the workplace adjustments described previously are a good first step here. Promoting good health is a great way to demonstrate the focus your organization has on employee wellness. Management capable of identifying the subtle signs of employees who are dealing with small health issues that can impact their productivity is another vital element. When your staff can intervene and help employees find effective healthcare solutions as quickly as possible, they send the message that being in the office and as healthy as possible is the ideal. This, in turn, encourages employees to take care of themselves while still returning to work as soon as they can. And in the meantime, remote work can ensure that their absence is not felt too keenly.

What is the overall takeaway from this information? First, both absenteeism and presenteeism have a massive negative impact on productivity and financial stability. Second, both issues can be measured, so the company has the opportunity to fix or minimize them. The exact solutions you put into place will vary largely depending on your business and your work culture. One suggestion is to offer an incentive for perfect attendance—a monetary goal. Absenteeism and presenteeism, however, are unique to each company. There is an abundance of each. When you get the results of the metrics, review them with a specialist in this area. They will help you reduce both absenteeism and presenteeism.

Finally, keep the following in mind as you read further: There's a precise line that falls between working enough hours to be productive and working too many hours and becoming unproductive. In fact, the term *counterproductive* derives from one's continuing to work past the moment of productivity.

The Business Case
Cost of Absenteeism

Earlier in this chapter, I briefly discussed the cost of absenteeism. According to workforce solution company Circadian, unscheduled absenteeism costs roughly $3,600 per year for each hourly worker and $2,650 each year for salaried employees. Even a 1 percent or half a percent decrease in absenteeism can reduce those costs.

1. Take the example of 1,000 employees with an average absenteeism rate of 3 percent (1,000 x 3 percent = 30).
2. On any given day, 30 employees are absent.
3. Multiply 30 by an estimated $3,000 per employee; you'll find that absenteeism is costing you $90,000 a day.
4. Multiply that by 260 workdays per year; this totals $23,400,000.
5. If you reduce the average absent day to 2.5 percent, and do the same calculations, absenteeism will cost you $19,500,000.
6. The savings to the company in this example is $3,900,000.

Absenteeism costs affect every type of employer in all industries. According to the Bureau of Labor Statistics 2019 survey on absenteeism, the private sector's overall absenteeism rates across all industries is 2.7 percent. The rate of full-time salaried and wage workers varies across industries and ranges from 1.7 percent in mining, quarrying, and oil and gas extraction to 3.3 percent in education and health services. Even managerial employees have a rate of nearly 2.5 percent. Sales and related occupations have a rate of 3.1 percent. The Bureau of Labor Statistics data includes time off from work for reasons such as illness, family leave, jury duty, civic duty, and maternity, but they do not include vacation time off.

The following table presents annual cost estimates of unscheduled absenteeism in various industries using the latest available industry-specific absenteeism rates given various cost per year per worker assumptions and assuming an employer with 1,000 employees, ranging from $2,500 in scenario 1, $2,650 in scenario 2, $3,000 in scenario 3, and $3,600 in scenario 4.

The last line of the table presents the annual savings in each scenario assuming a half-percent decrease in absenteeism. Even in the most conservative scenario, which assumes a cost of absenteeism per year per worker of only $2,500, the annual savings is $3,250,000.

Cost of Presenteeism

Popular reading suggests that presenteeism costs the organization 10 times more than absenteeism. Yet when I have searched for supporting documentation, I could not find any credible sources. Here is what I found:

According to an American Productivity Audit carried out using the Work and Health Interview, a telephone survey of a random sample of 28,902 US workers designed to quantify lost productive work time for personal and family health reasons and expressed in hours and dollars, health-related lost productive time costs employers $225.8 billion

	Average Absenteeism Rate	Scenario 1	Scenario 2	Scenario 3	Scenario 4
All private sector industries	2.7	17,550,000	18,603,000	21,060,000	25,272,000
Agriculture and related industries	2.1	13,650,000	14,469,000	16,380,000	19,656,000
Nonagricultural industries	2.7	17,550,000	18,603,000	21,060,000	25,272,000
Mining, quarrying, and oil and gas extraction	1.7	11,050,000	11,713,000	13,260,000	15,912,000
Construction	2.4	15,600,000	16,536,000	18,720,000	22,464,000
Manufacturing	2.5	16,250,000	17,225,000	19,500,000	23,400,000
Wholesale and retail trade	2.8	18,200,000	19,292,000	21,840,000	26,208,000
Transportation and utilities	2.8	18,200,000	19,292,000	21,840,000	26,208,000
Information	2.6	16,900,000	17,914,000	20,280,000	24,336,000
Financial activities	2.4	15,600,000	16,536,000	18,720,000	22,464,000
Professional and business services	2.4	15,600,000	16,536,000	18,720,000	22,464,000
Education and health services	3.3	21,450,000	22,737,000	25,740,000	30,888,000
Leisure and hospitality	3.0	19,500,000	20,670,000	23,400,000	28,080,000
Savings from a half a percent decrease in absenteeism		3,250,000	3,445,000	3,900,000	4,680,000

annually, or on average $1,685 per employee per year. Although the study found that costs vary significantly by worker characteristics such as gender, type of job, smokers versus nonsmokers, this average cost per employee per year can help provide a rough estimate of the cost of presenteeism.[*]

In the case of our example above—1,000 employees—disregarding actual workforce characteristics, the average annual cost estimate of presentism is $1,685,000 per year. This is the most conservative estimate I could find. There is reliable information that provides greater detail about the cost of presenteeism if the employer has data on certain conditions.[†] See Table 3A in this report which shows the average daily dollar impact of each condition. If you have a proper well-being program, this data would be readily available.

Also, a survey from the United Kingdom[‡] claims, "Research reveals today that three-quarters of ill-health-related productivity loss is due to factors which can be influenced and addressed through health and productivity management strategies." The cost estimate to the United Kingdom is £61 billion to £82 billion per year as a result of employees' ill health, which is 35.6 working days per employee, on average. Using the assumption we used previously, in an organization with 1,000 employees and an average salary of $75,000 per year, the loss of productivity is 13.6 percent payroll (35.6/261) which equals a loss to the firm of $10,200,000.

For further reading about absenteeism and presenteeism, see Appendix B.

---

[*]   Stewart, W., Ricci, J., Chee, E. and Morganstein, D., 2003. Lost Productive Work Time Costs from Health Conditions in the United States: Results from the American Productivity Audit. *Journal of Occupational and Environmental Medicine*, 45(12): 1234–1246.

[†]   Goetzel, R., Long, S., Ozminkowski, R., Hawkins, K., Wang, S. and Lynch, W., 2004. Health, Absence, Disability, and Presenteeism Cost Estimates of Certain Physical and Mental Health Conditions Affecting U.S. Employers. *Journal of Occupational and Environmental Medicine*, 46(4): 398–412.

[‡]   Work in Mind. 2019. Presenteeism & Ill Health: Cost to British Businesses Is £61 Billion a Year. [online] Available at: <https://workinmind.org/2019/04/15/presenteeeism-ill-health/>.

CHAPTER FOUR
Key Component #2—
Well-Being (Well-Zilience)

CEO: Today's discussion is likely a topic you're very familiar with: *well-being*, which some refer to as *wellness*. I prefer a new word: *well-zilience*. The other two terms have become somewhat outdated, in my opinion. Well-zilence captures staying healthy and bouncing back. Regardless of which term we use, what does this topic mean to you?

Bethany: Being sick.

Kent: Worry.

CEO: Worry about what?

Milton: Finances, marriage, relationships.

CEO: Exactly . . . and more. We spoke about being absent and not present—each affects productivity and even our happiness. There are many aspects to well-being. Today, I'm going to speak to those. Again, the goal is to improve people's lives. This is not altruistic. It's not my place to tell you how to improve your lives. But I do know that if you improve your lives, as each one of us must do in one way or another, it will make you happier. And if you're happier . . .

Milton: We'll be more productive.

CEO: And if we're more productive?

Kent: We will worry less.

CEO: Yes, and . . . ?

Bethany: We will make more money for the company?

CEO: Which will . . . ?

Mark: Make us more money.

CEO: Which will in turn . . . ?

Milton: Get me that boat I've always wanted.

Bethany: Or my summer home.

CEO: Whatever it is, it will improve your life. It's a win-win. You are healthier and happier, and the company is more productive, which increases revenue and profits. Those are profits I can share with the employees.

Socrates once said that "a life unexamined is a life unfulfilled." Freud had similar sentiments when he said that work and love are key components to happiness. Both of these insights are as relevant today as they were when these men were living. These insights are woefully missing in our organizations, as is made very clear in "The Sad State of Happiness in the United States and the Role of Digital Media" by Dr. Jean M. Twenge, Professor of Psychology at San Diego State University.

As our online time increases, our general happiness decreases. This is because we spend too much time neglecting our lives in favor of quick diversion. It is only when the focus shifts to an examination of our own life (re: Socrates) and we take action to balance it with work and love (re: Freud) that change occurs and life improves.

There are a few different types of well-being to keep in mind when you make the decision to examine your life and start changing it for the better. I will present five of them. These are applicable to anyone and everyone. As a CEO who experienced my own workplace burnout and depression, I have learned how important it is to understand these various areas. In this chapter, I explore each one of them, and I talk about how they've helped me both in my life and in business. And to provide even more support to the idea that change comes from within ourselves rather than from external forces alone, we'll take a look at some return on investment (ROI) studies at the end of the chapter.

Emotional and Physical Well-Being

The first kind of well-being deals with your mind. Your feelings are the foundation upon which a happy, balanced life is built. It starts in the mind and moves to the heart. And if you have this sector in tune, like a fine piano, all the other notes that create a happy life will be much easier to master. If it's not in tune, however, then it seems like nothing aligns quite right.

Mental health is important, and it's far too easy to overlook that in the rush of today's society. Sometimes it seems as though the world really does value the end product over the person. For example, there was always a place for me because I was a hard worker. The expression "hard work trumps everything" really worked to my benefit. I was bright enough that I could quickly learn things. With this powerful combination, the world was my oyster—or so I thought. I didn't stop to think about how my mental health might be impacting my social life and actually reducing my professional productivity, despite the fact that I was doing well.

So what if I couldn't hold on to a relationship? I didn't need one—I got my self-worth from my work. Of course, that took me only so far and was indicative of a deeper problem that I was all too happy to gloss over. It wasn't until I'd gone through a few failed relationships that I knew I needed help. My friend Danny offered to introduce me to his therapist. "Not for me," I said. My problems weren't that deep, and the stigma of going to a therapist was just too much to bear. But after even more emotional pain, and with the constant and beautiful friendship of Danny, who regularly pushed me to see someone, I went.

It changed my life. I completely respect those who have tried therapy and say it isn't for them. I've been there. I got lucky with my first encounter and found a really good therapist when I lived in New York. However, when I moved to Los Angeles and looked for a new therapist, it took me five years to find someone who worked well with me. The search was worth it. I discovered psychoanalysis, a deeper form of therapy. Bottom line: I'm in a healthy marriage and my income has increased tenfold since I started therapy. I'd consider that successful, wouldn't you? This incomprehensible level of productivity was evidence that there's more to living a successful life than just working harder. Through this, I learned that emotional well-being is the root and foundation for everything else. If you remember only one key piece of advice from this book, this is it: Take care of your emotional state first. It will lay the groundwork for greater life success and productivity.

Emotional well-being has also helped me identify many problems within organizations. As a consultant, I studied the culture of organizations, asking employees to complete confidential assessments for feedback about where their company could improve. As with people, some organizations are healthy and some are not. After I discovered that my income and overall sense of well-being were dependent on my emotional well-being, I applied the same concept to my clients' organizations. As I experimented with my own company by improving the well-being of my staff by providing empowerment, emotional tools, and opportunities to help themselves, the company rose to another level. I had a first-class seat from which to watch people become successful and healthier and to ultimately produce better work as a result. These are the same concepts I used in improving my own mental health: seeking out qualified therapy, asking myself questions, and becoming aware of the logic behind choices I had made. Investing in your mental health not only improves your life experience but also positively impacts your cash flow. And who wouldn't mind making more money while feeling better and potentially reducing workload in the process?

The second kind of well-being is short and straight to the point: your physical well-being. Paying attention to this improves your overall quality of life and can also impact your emotional health. Adopting any kind of healthier diet and active lifestyle, including just taking walks, has been scientifically proven to improve both mood and body and to produce both endorphins and dopamine. Both give you more energy and make you happier, so you want high levels of them in your brain. Healthy and fit people are happier people. And as we've discussed, emotional well-being has a direct impact on our productivity. Physical well-being, then, has quite a big impact on efficiency and your overall ability to get things done. If you are constantly not feeling well or are eating foods that weigh you down, you're less likely to do what must be done in both your personal life and your professional endeavors.

Adopting a healthier lifestyle doesn't have to be overwhelming. In fact, there are a few great ways to facilitate it. Incorporating a short walk at lunchtime, standing up during meetings, and exercising while listening to an audiobook, for example, all make strides in the right direction over the long term. I myself have realized that the more active I am, the more productive I tend to be. After I discovered this, I bought a treadmill desk. This equipment is exactly what it sounds like: a desk attached to a treadmill that enables the user to work and walk at the same time. I use my treadmill desk every day. I set the pace very slow—1.3 mph—and immediately start working. It doesn't take long to subconsciously forget that I'm walking. I generally walk on the treadmill portion from 1 to 3 hours daily; the remainder of the day, I stand up at the desk. In this way, I ensure that my lifestyle is active and that I promote my good health without interrupting my day or requiring much effort on my part. It is also a great way to accomplish multiple tasks at the same time. This is not multitasking in the traditional sense. Multitasking, per se, is actually impossible: your conscious mind cannot focus on two thoughts at the same time. People who appear to be multitasking are actually rapidly going back and forth between disparate tasks rather than completing multiple tasks simultaneously. Walking or standing while working, however, can become second nature. And because you are doing it subconsciously, you can focus on the work in front of you. You are truly accomplishing two tasks—upgrading your work performance and improving your physical health—at the same time.

Beyond your mental health, physical well-being impacts how well your body functions and for how long. The top three killers in the United States are heart disease, cancer, and respiratory diseases. Moderate exercise significantly reduces the risks for each of them. And even 2.5 hours of exercise per week can lead to a noticeable decline in absenteeism, according to a study by the *Journal of Occupational and Environmental Medicine*. Given that information, should employers encourage exercise at work? You bet!

Financial Well-Being

The third kind of well-being—financial well-being—correlates to the number-one stressor in many households. Only 35 percent of respondents reported satisfaction with their financial situation, as compared to 48 percent two years ago, according to the "Global Benefits Attitudes Survey" by Willis Towers Watson. That decrease makes sense given the overall declining financial wellness of people in modern society. That kind of stress impacts both your emotional and your physical well-being if it continues for long enough. The weight of financial burdens, if allowed to continue, can ruin the overall outcome of days, weeks, months, and years. I would ask companies to create a system that helps people improve their financial state. Whether they offer finance classes to help people make better decisions or they aid in loan repayment, it is their job to help people ease their financial worries. After all, this is the reason they come to work every day.

Financial stress might not seem like something that employers must concern themselves with. Many businesses still uphold the traditional idea that personal issues shouldn't impact work performance, and that very much includes money troubles. But the reality is that it is important to recognize financial distress, and to remedy it as much as possible, because it has a significant impact on worker productivity. As many as 80 percent of employers say that poor financial well-being diminishes the performance levels of their workforce,* leading to a loss of a half a trillion dollars every year.† Money concerns stem from various sources, some of which we've briefly touched upon—student debt, home loans, and poor retirement savings among them—and many workers simply don't feel as though they are in a place where they can easily address these issues. That means that they are constantly living in a haze of stress and worry, with no end in sight. It isn't difficult to see exactly how that negatively impacts their work performance.

The good news is that you can help your employees with their financial concerns without impacting your budget or bottom line. One of the best things you can do for your workforce is to establish a financial wellness education program to help teach your workers how to make the most out of their money and how to plan for the future. Taking the time to offer your employees the education they need in order to thrive is also a good way to boost company loyalty, creating employees who not only are unencumbered by serious financial worries but also are more engaged and productive due to dedication to their work and to the organization overall.

Beyond a financial literacy program, there are a few additional steps you can take that will help avoid serious problems before they begin. They will significantly impact the productivity of your workforce.

Fair Pay

Of course, the most obvious step to securing the financial success of your employees is to look at their salaries. Are they being paid a competitive wage? This is important for a few reasons. First, boosting the salary on an underpaid position can help solve many financial concerns right away. Even more than that, however, ensuring that your valued employees are being paid competitively helps reduce the chances of their leaving your organization in search of a company willing to pay them fair wages. Consider running periodic surveys of market rates for the positions represented in your company and make sure that they are in line with what you are offering.

---

* Miller, S., 2016. Employees' Financial Issues Affect Their Job Performance. [online] Shrm.org. Available at: <https://shrm.org/ResourcesAndTools/hr-topics/benefits/Pages/Employees-Financial-Issues-Affect-Their-Job-Performance.aspx>.

† Anderson, B., 2019. Panic Attack: Worker Financial Stress Costs Employers $500 Billion Annually. [online] 401K Specialist. Available at: <https://401kspecialistmag.com/panic-attack-worker-financial-stress-costs-employers-500-billion-annually>.

Open Communication

Financial concerns often leave people feeling ashamed and reluctant to reach out for help. It is important to put their minds at ease by offering judgment-free help when you notice their struggles. Don't wait for employees to come to you. By the time they finally reach out for resources, their situation is likely much worse than it would have been had you intervened earlier. And remember that the worse their situation is, the less productive your employees will be. Approach your workforce and ask how you can help. In fact, ask them how you might implement programs in the office to help prevent money issues in the future. Their responses often might be requests for increased pay, but you will likely gain insight into the concerns of your employees and how the organization helps or hinders them in the process.

Flexible Schedules

This particular step may be controversial. Despite the evidence that remote work and flexible schedules can lead to an increase in productivity, many companies are reluctant to even consider establishing them as viable options for their employees. It's important to remember that life doesn't always run on a 9-to-5 schedule. Sometimes offering flexible scheduling can enable employees to reduce expenses, such as childcare, and to be more focused in the office due to less concern about finances. Remote work can be a great option here as well, by giving workers the chance to build a schedule and workplace that best fits their needs. When employees are happy and are operating from an optimal place, both their production and engagement will improve. Flexible schedules and remote work options can have a massive impact on the overall well-being of your employees and on their financial well-being in particular.

Good Benefits

Make sure that you are providing your employees with the best benefits and incentives that you can. Working hard is easier when they have a goal to meet, especially when reaching it leads to tangible rewards rather than simply meeting a quota. Financial incentives will work the best in this situation, but other types of incentives can help improve productivity without necessarily impacting financial wellness. The goal is to encourage your workers to collectively improve their performance because they benefit from doing so.

Find the Right Financial Wellness Program

It's important to find the right program for your workplace. In general, it's likely that the best option is to reach out to a financial wellness firm and let the experts work with your employees. They have the time and resources to give your workers the custom help they need, along with a sense of privacy they might not feel when working directly with their managers or others within your organization. This strategy also helps reduce the potential drain on your internal resources that offering financial wellness education might have.

Financial wellness can be a delicate topic to tackle. However, it is a vital one to address as quickly as possible because the lack of wellness here is a major productivity killer.

Occupational Well-Being

It's important that you love what you do. This applies to your employees as well. Research shows that when people enjoy what they do, and when they work in the field they are passionate about while using the skills they are gifted with, their morale increases. And increased morale leads to heightened productivity. But not everyone is fortunate enough to find a job in the area they love. Help your employees discover their passion. Or perhaps their passion does not remunerate well enough to provide for their household. I know firsthand how frustrating that can be.

As a playwright and producer, writing and producing plays and movies is what I dreamed of doing. And though I did find time to write plays, I spent considerable time running my company. This is when I came up with the idea to work smart. I wanted to devote more time to creative arts and giving my inner soul enough room to breathe and expand, but I still had to provide for myself and my family. Stumbling into sales and finding my niche in corporate America utilized special talents I did not know I had. I then realized that I have a passion for helping people and doing that as much as I can every day has greatly improved my overall outlook on life.

What a person wants to do—what they've dreamed of doing—might not be something they can turn into a full-time career, but that doesn't mean they have to be miserable every day. A person looking to be more productive can try to find a career that fits their talents, interests, and skills. They can experiment with jobs in various industries, even if they don't think those jobs correlate with their skill set. Doing something a person is good at—and that they know they are good at—enhances their quality of life and gives them a stronger sense of purpose.

Social Well-Being

Finally, social well-being reflects the feeling that you are a part of something greater than yourself—a community—and gives you the drive to contribute to it. Being involved in a community expands your perspective, and that's one of the reasons I advise corporations to look at this as part of their culture. I ask the CEOs to question whether there is a presence of teamwork, of unity, and of a motivation to happily complete goals in their offices or if, instead, the environment is simple, boring, and unmotivating. There are a few things you can do to increase your knowledge in this area. Geert Hofstede's cultural dimensions theory, for example, is fascinating reading. His work describes the uniqueness of cultural values among countries. In short, there are significant differences in the respective cultures of countries. These can affect revenue and profits. I found the group culture present in many Asian countries to be very interesting in contrast with the individualized culture in the United States. A global CEO must be aware of these stark differences because they can make or break the firm. Here's a simple example: On the first day of work in the United States, the culture dictates placing an employee at a desk with a chair and a computer and then putting him or her to work. In Japan, they start employees in groups, not as individuals. If you force American corporate culture on acclimating employees in Japan, you will face a greater chance of losing them, whether to frustration or sheer confusion, and overall productivity will suffer.

Building a workforce that enjoys its work and is willing to go above and beyond the call of duty in order to help the organization grow doesn't rest solely on the workers' mental and physical health. Some of the most important factors are external, with the work environment having a big impact on employees' experiences there. Promoting a strong and supportive workplace culture is a vital element to encouraging employee engagement and success. This makes community wellness one of the most critical forms of wellness to keep in mind.

What Is Social Wellness?

Social wellness, or social well-being, is the idea of enjoying your workplace, having pride in it and in your coworkers, and feeling safe and secure every day when you go into work. In short, it's a term that calls attention to the concept of wellness as it pertains to an entire community. If the community is unwell or is lacking in some regard, one might find it difficult to be as productive as possible. But what exactly does an "unwell" community look like? There are a few things to examine. Consider the broader workplace community to be a reflection of the organization's inner workings and values. You'd hope to see a group of individuals who are passionate about their work, good at what they do, and dedicated to bettering themselves and their coworkers so that they might better support corporate growth. That is what a healthy community looks like. An unhealthy community is one in which employee relations with each other and with managers are fractured. Instead of trust and a genuine appreciation for organizational values, workers are pushed to labor on their own and to worry about their own progress, with a fear of chastisement or further punishment for any mistakes. The group is not united, it is not excited, and it is not passionate about self-improvement in the name of organizational growth.

You might wonder if community wellness actually has any kind of measurable impact upon productivity, job satisfaction, and engagement. The answer is that it is surprisingly important. According to data discussed by *Harvard Business Review (HBR)*, workers of various age-groups valued community in the workplace so highly that it was one of the top three elements they wanted to see in their workplaces.[*] And this wasn't just the case in a small set of data. Additional research supports *HBR*'s findings, with workplace needs and desires remaining largely consistent across age-groups and with social and community aspects ranking highly.[†] The bottom line is that employees of all ages highly value community in the workplace and cite it as an important factor influencing their job satisfaction and engagement. Achieving this can be as simple as fostering an environment where support

---

[*]   Goler, L., Grant, A., Harrington, B. and Gale, J., 2018. The 3 Things Employees Really Want: Career, Community, Cause. [online] Harvard Business Review. Available at: <https://hbr.org/2018/02/people-want-3-things-from-work-but-most-companies-are-built-around-only-one>.

[†]   Twenge, J., Campbell, S., Hoffman, B. and Lance, C., 2010. Generational Differences in Work Values: Leisure and Extrinsic Values Increasing, Social and Intrinsic Values Decreasing. *Journal of Management*, 36(5): 1117–1142.

and friendship are encouraged. Gallup finds that individuals with friends at work are twice as likely to feel engaged with their jobs as those without.* There are guidelines to follow if you want to create a workplace community that actively promotes engagement and job satisfaction, and they are more involved than simply encouraging employee friendship.

How Can I Improve Social/Community Well-Being?

One of the best ways to improve community well-being is to consult with the individuals working within that community. Instead of placing company leaders as figureheads who are in charge of shaping and driving the workplace, consider working with your employees instead. They stand to gain, or lose, the most from the environment and are best equipped to offer suggestions and ideas to further unify the workforce. Creating employee networks based on shared interests is a good way to encourage workers to take part in the community-building process and to get to know one another. Make sure you have program leaders who are able to review and assess the resulting networks to ensure that they reflect the diverse and inclusive culture that encourages unity.

You might also consider taking some time out of the normal schedule to plan community activities or cause-based activities. This doesn't require a lot of free time, nor must it be a daily occurrence, although you can certainly tie community building into daily wellness activities such as exercise classes. These activities or excursions can be based on shared recreational interests, professional interests, or cause-based interests. Promoting group activities based on these criteria is a good way to build bonds between workers and to enable the workforce community to grow and thrive. Allocating budget and time to these activities also helps employees understand that you care about their well-being, fostering an increased sense of loyalty and engagement.

Finally, consider making use of social media platforms. Don't worry, I'm not suggesting that everyone spend hours on Facebook every day while at work. I'm talking about utilizing communication applications such as Slack or Yammer, both of which are designed to unite work communities and to make it easy for employees to organize events and for employers to supervise

---

*   Mann, A., 2018. Why We Need Best Friends at Work. [online] Gallup.com. Available at: <https://www.gallup.com/workplace/236213/why-need-best-friends-work.aspx>.

them and keep tabs on community growth. If you decide to take this route, make sure that you regularly monitor these platforms for misuse.

Social well-being does not have to be difficult to achieve. You can meet most of these guidelines by combining efforts with other wellness initiatives, such as exercise classes or professional growth training. When you promote a sense of community based on shared values, you're encouraging your employees to understand the importance of working together to reach shared goals and to draw support from one another to excel in their day-to-day activities. This kind of relationship can do much to boost the overall productivity and engagement of a workforce, driving performance higher while creating an environment that nurtures and maintains talent while building strong ties with corporate values and goals. This is one of the most important areas of wellness you can emphasize if you're hoping to optimize employee engagement.

The health of the community determines whether a company is a great place to work. As a CEO and business advisor, I recommend that management usher in the environment they want to create. If a company occasionally treats its staff to lunch, it satisfies two kinds of employee well-being: physical and financial. The firm will see an immediate and measurable improvement in employee morale and productivity.

There is proof that all this works. The following sources have reported a higher ROI for employers after they have increased employee wellness and well-being:

- In 2010, Harvard University reported $3.00 in healthcare savings for every $1.00 spent on wellness and $3.00 in reduced absenteeism for every $1.00 invested.
- In 2012, Gallup reported that employers with well-being programs had 41 percent lower healthcare costs.
- The RAND Corporation found that employers save money mostly through disease management and correlated this to an overall well-being program.
- A WHO/WEF report estimates the economic benefit of scaling "best buy" interventions for noncommunicable diseases (NCDs). For example, in the United States alone, smoking causes $193 billion in health-related costs.

- At PepsiCo, over a seven-year period, employees who participated in both the lifestyle and disease management components of the corporate wellness program experienced an average reduction of $30 in healthcare costs per member per month. The disease management part of the wellness program was especially effective from a financial returns perspective. The study found that for every dollar invested in disease management, the return was $3.78.

Value of investment (VOI), a newer metric, has also been supported by the Business Group on Health. The metrics for measuring value for employers should include absenteeism, worker morale, employee turnover, recruitment, presenteeism, workers compensation, short- and long-term disability, employee engagement, loyalty and tenure, work safety accidents, and health savings. Valuing these metrics begins at a baseline; subsequently, measurements take place every six months. These improvements for employees increase worker productivity as well.

I encourage you to do a little digging within yourself and your company to discover how you can improve your firm using these five approaches to well-being. Some results take a little more time to surface than others, but proper measurement will enable you to see a tremendous difference.

The Business Case

There are various schools of thought on the ROI of wellness programs. This is sometimes controversial. Some professionals in the field believe that there are no ROIs on well-being or wellness programs. Others find it extremely helpful and show a strong ROI. One fact is clear: These programs must be designed carefully and specifically for each organization and its culture. If not, it will certainly fail.

According to recent RAND research, the larger the employer, the higher the likelihood of implementing a wellness program. Approximately one in three employers with 50 to 100 employees—and 80 percent of employers with 1,000 or more—offer wellness programs for their employees. According to a United Healthcare survey, employers' responses indicated that the ROI for wellness programs ranged between $1 and $4 for every dollar invested.

Typically, for every $1 spent on a wellness program, a company saves approximately $3 in health expenditures.

According to the Kaiser Family Foundation, a leading healthcare public policy nonprofit, the average annual employer-provided health insurance policy amounted to $7,188 for single coverage in 2019. Employers pay 82 percent of the premium on average, or $5,946. For family coverage, the average annual policy amounted to $20,576, with employers paying 70 percent on average, or $14,561.

Assuming the employer in our example provides single coverage for 500 of its employees and family coverage for the remaining 500 employees, the employer's total cost of providing health insurance is equal to $10,253,500 (that is, 500 x $5,946 + 500 x $14,561).

Wellness programs typically cost employers between $36 and $90 per employee per year. Given that for every $1 invested in such programs, the employer's health expenditures decrease by $3, the employer in our example could reduce its total annual cost of providing health insurance from $10,253,500 to $9,983,500, or by about $270,000.

As more companies try the programs, they are noticing a quick ROI from those initial costs. A survey from United Healthcare asked employers what their ROI was for wellness programs. The lowest reported ROI was a $1 return for every dollar spent, while others reported $4 for every dollar put into the program.[*]

For further reading about well-being, see Appendix C.

---

[*] Olsen, J., 2019. How Much Do Employee Wellness Programs Cost? | Passport Health. [online] Passporthealthusa.com. Available at: <https://www.passporthealthusa.com/employer-solutions/blog/2019-5-how-much-do-wellness-programs-cost/>.

CHAPTER FIVE
Key Component #3—
Engagement

CEO: When we last met, we spoke about *wellness* and *well-being*. Prior to that, we talked about *absence management* and *presenteeism*. These naturally lead to today's session, which is about *engagement*, which is perhaps the single biggest boost to productivity. I'll talk about myself and about how much time I'm honestly disengaged at work—and I'm the CEO. Let's be honest with each other here. What percentage of the time do you think you're actually engaged in work? Let's use the assumption that 100 percent would mean that you are fully engaged in your work 8 hours a day. I'll go first. I believe I'm about 80 percent engaged. Anybody care to comment?

Kent: It depends on the day and how I feel. Some days I'll come in and be as much as 80 percent engaged; on other days, I might be engaged as little as 50 percent of the time.

Bethany: I feel the same way. But to be honest, I don't know that I can say that I'm ever 100 percent engaged.

Milton: Me too. I don't slack off, that's for sure. It's important for me as a manager to set an example for others, but there certainly are times when I'm surfing the net or taking too long of a coffee break or a longer lunch than maybe is best for the company.

CEO: That's terrific. Very honest and exactly what I'm looking for. Each percentage increase of our engagement will have a direct effect on our top line. As you know, if the top line grows, so will our bottom line. Thanks for being honest with me. Let's dig into this topic more deeply. It's very important.

Employee engagement is an approach to the workplace that actively promotes high productivity and job satisfaction. It is vital to the success of a business as well as to each employee's ability to thrive professionally as well as privately. Even more than that, however, employee engagement is how you measure your employees' commitment to your firm's values and goals as well as their desire and motivation to contribute to your company's success.

This is an important component to keep in mind if you're hoping to create the most productive workplace possible and to minimize both presenteeism and absenteeism, two issues that are detrimental to an office's overall morale and output. If you create an environment in which your employees are motivated and excited to work, they will go above and beyond to ensure that everything they do is as complete and high quality as possible. This will translate into better service to customers, increased productivity, and subsequently to higher revenue and profits.

With that said, the topic can sometimes be confusing to understand. Employee engagement is often mistaken for job satisfaction. It's related, but is not the same thing. Because it's such an indispensable part of a healthy work environment, I will take some time to look at employee engagement more closely before we dive into the metric itself. I will also examine ways to establish engagement-boosting workplace strategies.

Employee Engagement Versus Job Satisfaction

To be clear, employee satisfaction does not indicate employee engagement. Although the two might go hand in hand with each other, it is necessary to understand the difference between the two terms in order to effectively address both issues. If you're interested in determining how happy workers are in their jobs, then you'll want to look specifically at employee satisfaction. But understand that highly satisfied employees are not always highly engaged employees. For many, securing financial well-being might be enough to be "satisfied" with a job for which they might otherwise feel no particular passion or motivation. As long as employees with this view are getting paid for their work, then they're likely to rank their satisfaction with their position highly regardless of how much they care about the organization, its products, and its values.

The main difference between satisfied employees and engaged employees is emotional attachment. While the traditional approach to encouraging high performance from employees is to chastise for mistakes and punish for unfulfilled quotas, it is far more effective to foster a good relationship with employees through compassionate management and quality benefits that enable them to thrive. Doing this can often result in engaged employees—workers who not only enjoy their work but also appreciate the company for which they work. They believe that their work is important and that if they stopped performing so highly, their actions would negatively impact the company. These employees are far more likely than others to go above and beyond what is expected of them to ensure their work is excellent and that their contributions are genuinely helpful. They also often hope to advance in their current company to cultivate a long-term career.

Satisfied employees, on the other hand, are not emotionally bonded with their work or their company. They are happy with what they are doing and don't mind coming into work every day, leading them to be fairly productive and amenable. This is not the same as an employee who believes in the values their company is promoting, however, and they are generally happy enough to complete the work expected of them with minimal effort. And while engaged employees are connected with the workforce community and strive to build lasting professional relationships, satisfied employees are content to skip office activities in favor of quietly completing their tasks as quickly as possible.

Both satisfied employees and engaged employees are preferable to employees who are unmotivated and struggle to focus. However, the latter is more productive than the former. Engaged employees genuinely enjoy their time at work and set goals they want to achieve. They also won't hesitate to put in extra hours if necessary to excel and to meet even unexpected deadlines.

For these reasons, improving job satisfaction is a good step to take, but it is not a step that necessarily increases performance. And because satisfaction doesn't always translate into passionate, ambitious workers, having an alternate method of measurement is important. That's where employee engagement comes in. Employee engagement focuses not on how much employees like their jobs but rather on how compelled they feel to do well in their position. Workers who feel strongly about their industry and their organization—those who believe in the values and mission their company holds—are highly motivated to give their best every day. And this is far more likely to drive performance than is satisfaction alone.

The following are among the many factors that influence an employee's level of engagement with their work as well as with the company as a whole:

- Good leadership that encourages compassionate management
- Regular communication between management and employees
- Empowering employees to take risks
- Empowering employees to make decisions
- Regular performance assessments for feedback
- An open and safe work environment
- Management that cares about its employees

If you can implement some of these initiatives, employees will be more engaged. And if they are more engaged, you should see in them some of these qualitative results:

- A sense of pride in working for the organization
- An interest in promoting the organization as a great place to work
- A lack of interest in other job opportunities
- A strong sense of job satisfaction
- A feeling that one's work strongly contributes to the organization's success
- A feeling that is compelled by the organization's mission to make a difference
- A willingness to put in more effort than is expected

Employee engagement impacts both employees and organizations on many different levels. In order to gain as many benefits as possible, careful attention is required to identify and strengthen the employee's interest in engagement.

Why Is Employee Engagement Important?

According to the *Harvard Business Review* (*HBR*),[*] there are a few reasons why employee engagement is a top priority for executives. First, today's society moves very quickly, with new technology and techniques constantly

---

[*] 2013. *The Impact of Employee Engagement on Performance.* [ebook] Available at: <https://hbr .org/resources/pdfs/comm/achievers/hbr_achievers_report_sep13.pdf>.

being created to meet the evolving demands of consumers in all industries. To stay on top of the field and ensure the growth and success of a business, innovation and productivity must be encouraged. If employees are unable to generate new ideas, adapt to new technology or new demands, and thrive even as their industry changes, then the business itself will find it more difficult to strengthen and grow. Employee engagement separates workers who are dedicated to creating the best business possible from those who are simply interested in a paycheck. It encourages growth and good performance.*

Employee engagement is also important in slowing employee turnover and retaining talent. If your workers feel strongly about your company and believe that their contribution is important, they are much less likely to leave their role. This is something that might not have seemed quite as urgent a few decades ago, but time has greatly changed the professional landscape. Instead of finding positions that employees intend to fill for the duration of their careers, "mobile" careers are far more common. This means that employees are more likely to move around until they find the perfect fit for their beliefs and abilities. Top talent will generally have little trouble landing new positions, even when employment rates are down for an industry, because businesses are always looking for innovative team members to help give them a competitive edge.

Employee engagement can help minimize or avoid employee retention issues. When workers feel strongly about a specific organization and are highly involved in its business and its culture, they are less likely to actively seek new positions elsewhere. If you're hoping to hold on to your high performers while also maximizing their output and the quality of their work, it's vital to examine employee engagement and ensure that it's optimized.

The Proof

Several in-depth studies regarding employee engagement have been conducted. In a report compiled by the *HBR*,† at least 550 executives—including 12 best-practice industry leaders—were interviewed regarding their feelings

---

*   Sorenson, S., 2013. How Employee Engagement Drives Growth. [online] Gallup.com. Available at: <https://www.gallup.com/workplace/236927/employee-engagement-drives-growth .aspx>.

†   2013. *The Impact of Employee Engagement on Performance.* [ebook] Available at: <https://hbr .org/resources/pdfs/comm/achievers/hbr_achievers_report_sep13.pdf>.

about employee engagement. The results were eye-opening on various levels. Of the 550 executives interviewed, 71 percent thought that employee engagement was vital to achieving and maintaining overall organizational success. Another study, published in 2016, found a direct link between organizational innovation and employee engagement.[*] Researchers found that the two issues reinforce each other, with engaged staff more likely to be innovative than those who were not.

These studies also found that, despite its importance, leaders are not doing enough to drive employee engagement. When questioned about current engagement policies or strategies, *HBR* found that only 24 percent of respondents felt their employees were highly engaged at work. Perhaps even more important, *HBR* also found that executives were far more optimistic about the level of engaged workers in their business than were the direct superiors of those workers. Company leaders must be as engaged as their employees regarding understanding their workplace culture and the challenges that managers see in frontline workers. Paying attention to your employees and implementing practices that promote their engagement are important steps to take.

Employee Engagement and Presenteeism

We know from previous chapters that presenteeism is a big issue that has a dramatic impact on workplace productivity and efficiency. When your employees are present but not engaged, you're looking at a form of presenteeism. This means that your workforce is physically present but not necessarily mentally focused. Their work suffers and, as a result, your business suffers. Employee engagement can help change that.

It's important that employees use their strengths every day. When they do, they typically experience an 8 percent increase in their productivity. In addition, these workers are six times more likely to be productive and engaged with their work and their organization. To help ensure that these strengths are identified and utilized, businesses should also pay attention to middle management. Research shows that increasing the number of talented managers supervising employees, and subsequently doubling the number of engaged employees, can lead to an average of 147 percent

---

[*] Rao, V., 2016. *Innovation Through Employee Engagement*. [ebook] Second Asia Pacific Conference on Advanced Research. Available at: <https://apiar.org.au/wp-content/uploads/2016/05/APCAR_BRR710_BUS1-9.pdf>.

higher earnings per share than competition that doesn't.[*] About $7 trillion is lost annually due to diminished productivity that stems from the fact that 85 percent of employees are actively disengaged or are not otherwise focused at work.[†]

Communication is highly important. Organizations that seek to engage their workforce via employee communications applications software tend to see a 16 percent boost in employee productivity.[‡] This improves the overall worker experience that your company offers. Organizations scoring in the top quarter for employee experience receive almost three times the return on their assets and at least double their return on sales when compared to organizations that score in the bottom quarter.[§] Keep in mind that employee retention is improved with employee engagement. This is particularly important because 51 percent of all employees are actively looking for a new job or are keeping their eye out for openings. Companies with engaged employees can outperform those without by 202 percent.[¶]

Measuring Employee Engagement

You can't fix something without knowing what's wrong or how you're doing. That's why measuring employee engagement is important. There are a few different ways to go about this.

Surveys

Conducting surveys is a good way to measure employee engagement, but they must be the *right* surveys. Habitual and generic surveys are far less effective than dynamic surveys. Carefully craft engagement surveys that pertain

---

[*] Flade, P., Elliot, G. and Asplund, J., 2015. Employees Who Use Their Strengths Outperform Those Who Don't. [online] Gallup.com. Available at: <https://www.gallup.com/workplace/236561/employees-strengths-outperform-don.aspx>.

[†] Harter, J., n.d. Dismal Employee Engagement Is a Sign of Global Mismanagement. [online] Gallup.com. Available at: <https://www.gallup.com/workplace/231668/dismal-employee-engagement-sign-global-mismanagement.aspx>.

[‡] 2019. *Dynamic Signal 2019 Customer Impact Study*. [ebook] Available at: <https://resources.dynamicsignal.com/ebooks-guides/dynamic-signal-2019-customer-impact-study>.

[§] n.d. *The Financial Impact of a Positive Employee Experience*. [ebook] Available at: <https://www.ibm.com/downloads/cas/XEY1K26O>.

[¶] Katz, E., 2017. Remote Workforce NPS: The Most Important Metric You're Missing. [online] Business 2 Community. Available at: <http://www.business2community.com/business-innovation/remote-workforce-nps-important-metric-youre-missing-01785305#oWRIA4bsxOwz6011.97>.

to your workforce and offer clear, pointed questions designed to look beyond job satisfaction. When you have that data in hand, review it and consider what it means for your workforce as well as your organization and whether you should be doing more to boost engagement in your business.

Goal Alignment

Employees who find that different supervisors have different goals for the company are more likely to feel confused and frustrated about their purpose than those whose workplace offers clear, consistent goals across the board. That means that the goals you personally hold as a CEO should be the goals that you share with your employees—the goals for which they are given the tools to succeed. You set those objectives, your managers should be creating specific objectives that align with those for individual employees, and those employees in question should have the autonomy and knowledge to meet the goals set before them.

Data Collection and Analysis

I mentioned the idea of conducting surveys and using data, but it's important enough to merit its own discussion. Measure productivity, performance, and engagement often. Use the data from your engagement surveys to develop initiatives, and even revise policy when necessary, to boost the metric as much as possible. Performance and productivity should be measured both before you send out surveys and after you make any of the changes. This will inform you as to whether your efforts are working as well as to whether or not you might need to develop additional engagement solutions.

Following these measurement tactics will help paint an accurate picture of engagement in your workforce.

Factors That Impact Engagement

Employee engagement is vital to an organization's success, but it doesn't necessarily take effect immediately. In fact, boosting employee engagement can become quite involved and take considerable time and resources to be effective. But the process doesn't have to be a complete mystery. There are several factors that consistently impact employee engagement across a wide array of fields and job titles. Here are some of the most common factors that impact engagement.

Expectations

If you expect your workforce to perform well and do their jobs effectively, you must first ensure that they understand exactly what is expected of them as well as the tools they have at their disposal to complete tasks. This is an important driving factor of engagement that can fairly easily make or break an employee's desire to go above and beyond to take care of the organization. Make sure that your expectations are very clear. Employees should know what they are supposed to do as well as their specific job responsibilities. Workers must also know about the tools available to them in fulfilling their responsibilities. Is the technology they're using up to date with industry standards? One of the biggest frustrations that can impede engagement and productivity is old technology that simply doesn't work as well as it should. Invest in the best tools possible for your employees so that they can meet and exceed your expectations. Not only do employers have expectations of their employees, but employees also have expectations of their employers. Most workers expect to have the technology and tools they need to succeed. When they can easily utilize these tools and complete their work as smoothly as possible, it is far easier to become engaged with the job and the tasks they're completing.

Contributions

Engaged employees contribute a lot to their organizations. Because they feel an emotional connection to their work, they are more likely than unengaged employees to put in the extra effort needed to take a project from "fine" to "outstanding." Before they can become engaged with the workplace, however, employees must understand that not only are they contributing to the organization but also that the organization is contributing to them. There are a few ways to go about this; we've already discussed one of them, compassionate productivity. Compassionate productivity can go a long way toward ensuring the workforce that their employers care about their well-being and their progress. Counsel your managers to be caring in their interactions with employees, including encouraging improvement and complimenting good work. In addition, engaged employees are often focused on doing the best they can and ascending in their fields. Contribute toward this goal—and foster loyalty to the organization—by offering these employees opportunities for professional development and growth.

Community

Community is a particularly important factor for engaged employees. In a rather stark contrast with satisfied employees, who generally have no problem keeping to themselves at work and checking out from the workforce community entirely, engaged employees actively enjoy their coworkers. They seek to build relationships with them, crafting a support group that exists for the benefit of everyone involved. Work is more than just a building where they spend a large portion of their life during the workweek. It becomes something more akin to a second home, filled with people with whom they enjoy working. These employees not only thrive on their community but also contribute to it in any way they can. This includes speaking up and voicing concerns, encouraging each other to do better, and celebrating organizational achievements because they genuinely care about their work. Building a workforce in which employees are encouraged to socialize when appropriate and to be friendly with one another is a great way to foster engagement and to build strong attachments both with their coworkers and to the company.

Growth

I mentioned this briefly before, but it's an important point that warrants elaboration. Engaged employees love their job and want to succeed. This includes climbing the ranks and ascending as far as they can, and they relish the opportunity to further develop their professional skills. Your organization should be ready and willing to offer them opportunities for growth and advancement. This includes a wide variety of activities, from attending conferences and trade shows to seeing a viable path to advancement within the company. Focus on investing resources in your engaged employees to help them grow and further strengthen their bond with the organization.

A Note About Leadership

Fostering employee engagement is vital in today's competitive global market, and it's important to utilize any possible advantage to do so. Leadership is one of the areas you should regularly evaluate when measuring employee engagement and developing a plan to increase it. Studies have shown that certain types of leadership are more effective at boosting engagement than others. Transformational leadership is generally the best choice. Employees who relate to their leaders and have strong relationships with them are more likely to become engaged with their work and workforce. This is due in large part to the personal relationship and trust that transformational leaders foster with their employees by inspiring them to improve in their position and motivating them to further develop their professional skills. It is interesting that transformational leaders are viewed not necessarily as power figures but rather as support systems that work for the collective good of the organization and for the workforce in question. This might play into the importance of community for engaged workers, with transformational leaders fitting into the community structure rather than existing outside it as looming authority figures.

Building trust and strong relationships between employees and managers is a good way to encourage engagement and strengthen an employee's connection with the organization itself. Every employee under a transformational leader will not necessarily become an engaged employee, but they will have a better chance than if they were working with a different leadership style. Taking the time to evaluate the leadership styles prevalent in your organization is a good way to optimize the company for engaged workers. You want to create a community and culture that encourages employees to do well and to connect with their coworkers and the values the organization promotes. It makes sense that more personal leadership styles play an important role.

This doesn't mean that every leader in the organization must have this kind of leadership style, but it is helpful if those who interact directly with the general workforce meet the description. The goal is to ensure that employees interact with leaders who genuinely care about them and their success and are able to communicate that effectively. Accomplishing this will give your company a head start on developing emotional bonds with employees who want to help the organization succeed.

It's time to focus on building a supportive community that promotes trust and loyalty in employees and their supervisors. This idea might seem rather novel to more traditional professionals familiar with established business practices, but it is absolutely vital to overcome hesitation. Today's world is not the same as it was even a decade or two ago, and it is imperative to encourage your business to grow and transform along with the outside world.

Engagement Tips

Making the decision to invest in employee engagement is a smart move, but it's not necessarily the easiest first step to take. In this instance, as with most things, the simple way is often the best. Talk to your employees and ask them what is standing in the way of engagement. Is there a specific policy or miscommunication serving as a barrier? Your employees are perhaps the best equipped to offer suggestions regarding workplace engagement, including ideas about what would increase it and how to change the overall office environment into one that encourages engagement and innovation. When you have these ideas, look them over with the other leaders and managers in your business and consider which are viable and how you would implement them.

Managers play an important role in employee engagement. Make sure you're hiring people who are willing and able to work with employees to set objectives that boost engagement. They should be able to recognize employee strengths and develop strategies to leverage them into organizational productivity and success. If your managers are unyielding and unapproachable, you're already facing a massive barrier to employee engagement. Coach them in the art of employee engagement and make that a metric by which their own performance is measured. Encourage them to do everything they can to give your frontline employees the tools they need to succeed.

There are a few more specific things to look into in order to boost employee engagement. First, make sure everyone you hire and manage is in the right role. Sometimes responsibilities change over time, often unintentionally, to pick up some of the slack left behind by a missing coworker or something similar. Over time, those responsibilities and tasks can add up and significantly change the scope of an employee's job. This is a problem, especially when they were hired for a particular talent. Make sure that your workforce is matched with the right tasks and expectations that maximize their interests and strengths. Employees who are interested in their work are much more likely to actively engage with it than those who are simply passing the time.*

---

* Gleeson, B., 2017. 5 Powerful Steps to Improve Employee Engagement. [online] *Forbes*. Available at: <https://www.forbes.com/sites/brentgleeson/2017/10/15/5-powerful-steps-to-improve-employee-engagement/#2d25bed8341d>.

Then, make sure everyone is properly trained.[*] You cannot reasonably expect your workforce to take responsibility for their success or failure when they haven't been trained in their positions. Give your employees the tools they need to succeed and thrive. Set them up for success and watch their engagement and productivity skyrocket. And make sure they're working on meaningful projects.[†] One of the worst things you can do is hire someone with great credentials and then hand them busywork because you don't yet have a position for them. Hire for the openings you have and ensure that everyone is working on projects specific to their roles.

Stay connected with your employees. Reach out and ask how they're doing and how they feel about their work. Give regular feedback. Don't wait until there is a serious issue that requires course correction. The more open and responsive you are, the happier and more engaged your workers will be.[‡]

One of the firms that I work for conducted an independent engagement survey across 20 countries and 26,000 employees. Many important results came out of the survey. First, 15 percent of the employees did not respond. This indicated clearly that 15 percent of the workforce was totally disengaged. Those who did respond commented on lack of communication from management to employees. They mentioned increased expectations from management from year to year without commensurate compensation. They also cited a constant sense of management urgency regarding increasing sales and revenue that garnered little interest among employees when it was announced, thereby leading to loss of respect from the employees as well as loss of engagement.

So far, we haven't discussed knowledge management much. In the survey, employees commented on the difficulty of finding people in the organization who were skilled at answering their compelling questions. No knowledge management system was in place. The company CEO reviewed the results with great concern and believed them. He didn't just bury his head in the sand. He wanted to make changes, so he asked that managers communicate

---

[*]   U, A. and W, P., 2015. Diving Deep in Employee Training to Understand Employee Engagement. *Business and Economics Journal*, 07(01).

[†]   Kahn, W. and Fellows, S., n.d. Employee engagement and meaningful work. *Purpose and Meaning in the Workplace*, pp. 105–126.

[‡]   Yohn, D., 2019. Employee Feedback Is Good for Employee Engagement; Action Is Better. [online] *Forbes*. Available at: <https://www.forbes.com/sites/deniselyohn/2019/08/06/employee-feedback-is-good-for-employee-engagement-action-is-better/#7b6f344b74cc>.

more regularly, implemented a knowledge management system so employees could access the wealth of knowledge in the firm, provided managers with training, spoke more to the employees through videos, traveled to more locations to generate engagement, reviewed the compensation programs to provide incentives to high performers, and tried to move an enormous organization in another direction. It worked. A dynamic and impressive CEO can take negative feedback about their organization, make positive and consistent changes, and transform their enterprise while achieving profitable results. A strong leader is all it takes.

I encourage you to take the time to measure your employees' engagement levels and implement carefully developed solutions to boost them. If you're hoping to see your business grow and succeed, this is a vital metric. Even more than that, it is a great way to boost both productivity and worker morale, ensuring that everyone in the office is happier and more willing to go above and beyond to make things happen.

The Business Case

Here are two examples that illustrate the many benefits of improving engagement:

Savings from reduced staff-turnover costs
Assume the following:
    a. A company of 1,000 employees.
    b. Average annual salary of $75,000/employee.
    c. Average annual turnover costs of 20 percent* of annual salary.
    d. Annual turnover rate of 20.1 percent (voluntary and involuntary).

Under these assumptions:
    e. Average turnover cost/person = $15,000.
    f. 201 employees lost annually.
    g. Cost to the company: $15,000 x 201 employees = $3,015,000 annually.

---

*   Boushey, H. and Glynn, S., 2012. There Are Significant Business Costs to Replacing Employees—Center for American Progress. [online] Center for American Progress. Available at: <https://www.americanprogress.org/issues/economy/reports/2012/11/16/44464/there-are -significant-business-costs-to-replacing-employees/>.

Recall that increasing employee engagement reduces annual turnover by 66 percent.[*] Reduction of turnover by 66 percent diminishes the $3,015,000 to $1,025,100. Total savings are $1,989,900.

Savings from reduced absenteeism costs
Based on research conducted by SHRM, companies with a gamification-focused employee engagement strategy reduced absenteeism by 24 percent.[†]

Assume the following:

   a. A company of 1,000 employees.
   b. Employees work 260 days a year.
   c. Absenteeism rate of 3 percent (see Chapter 3) is reduced by 24 percent to 2.28 percent via a gamification strategy; on any given day, 22.8 are absent (instead of the previous 30 employees).
   d. At this reduced rate, absenteeism costs the company $68,400 a day (22.8 x $3,000).
   e. Multiply that by 260 workdays per year; the company's cost of absenteeism is $17,784,000.
   f. This compares to $23,400,000 (Chapter 3) in the costs of absenteeism without a gamification strategy aimed at increasing engagement.
   g. This results in a savings of $5,616,000 from reduced absenteeism simply by implementing a gamification strategy to enhance employee engagement.

Total savings to a company with 1,000 employees: $1,989,900 + $5,616,000 = $7,605,900.

For further reading about engagement, see Appendix D.

---

[*]   imercer. 2020. North American Employee Turnover: Trends and Effects. [online] Available at: <https://www.imercer.com/articleinsights/North-American-Employee-Turnover-Trends-and-Effects>.
[†]   Hsu, K., 2016. 4 Ways to Calculate Employment Engagement ROI | Training Magazine. [online] Trainingmag.com. Available at: <https://trainingmag.com/4-ways-calculate-employment-engagement-roi/>.

CHAPTER SIX
Key Component #4—Technology

CEO: It's frustrating that I find my life choices are driven by technology. I feel that I'm losing more and more control of my own life to technology. My mind has been seduced to follow my smartphone. My computer drives my business. I have trouble reading the newspaper now. I opt instead for a quick fix on the Internet. Technology drives me; I don't drive it. Granted, these technological tools are designed to improve our lives—phones, toasters, televisions, computers—but for me, they've slowly and insidiously manifested themselves as part of my total being. It's now become so part of my life that I honestly don't know what I'd do without technology. Sounds like a sad state of mind, doesn't it? Well, it is in some respects. In other respects, it is here to stay and only promises to get more entrenched in our lives. Artificial intelligence, the next frontier, will take more decisions out of our own hands and into computers. Our businesses will be run by IBM's Watson before we know it. Regardless, as I said, it's here to stay and will only grow. So, let's take the bull by the horns—not buck the tide—and apply technology to our best purposes. Let's talk about the use of technology and how it can improve our work and our lives.

Milton: Or detract from both.

CEO: Exactly. Thank you, Milton. For the purposes of our discussion, let's define technology as any tool that has been developed to improve our performance. We'll also discuss how technology detracts from it. Let's take the smartphone for example. It's a great tool to improve our performance, right? How?

Bethany: To check emails.

Kent: Texts.

Milton: Simple access to a phone, wherever you are, to manage a business call.

CEO: And in our personal lives?

Kent: To be there for our families.

Bethany: (smiling) To make dinner reservations quickly or to get takeout.

CEO: To me, most important, it's helpful for emergencies. It has saved many lives. The smartphone is an amazing device. There are also some areas where it can be harmful. Studies show that looking at a phone—particularly for children—creates dopamine in the brain. Dopamine is a stimulant. There's a reason why we look at our phones quite often. Our brain gets stimulated from it, and this feels good. The same happens when you go to your favorite website or social media. All of this falls under the umbrella of technology, but it is not the kind of technology that will improve your performance. In fact, social media can lead to eyestrain and even depression. So what's the best way to use technology in the workplace? Let's explore.

The fifth key component to take into consideration is somewhat different from the previous four. We've talked about employee presenteeism and absenteeism and how each affects workplace productivity as well as how well-being and engagement can help minimize them. The next topic, however, is less about managing your employees' health and interest in their work and more about maximizing, through the use of strategic tools, what they complete while they're working. Assuming that the four previous components are present in your workplace, this one addresses how you can supplement those best practices with technology.

You might find my approach to incorporating technology into the workday surprising. With all of the apps and programs that profess to maximize productivity and improve focus, it would be logical to think I'd recommend a wide array of them to help bolster employee engagement. In reality, however, it's better to look at the apps and programs available for your industry and to carefully select a few that truly make your employees' lives easier.

I'd recommend just two or three productivity applications: an email app, an app that makes locating and parsing data easy—including knowledge management—and a task app. Keep in mind that more complex doesn't always mean "better," and that's especially true at work. You want your employees to focus on working on their projects or tasks rather than getting distracted by switching through multiple apps. Every app added to the workday also adds potential stumbling blocks to optimal performance. To maximize your returns, you must minimize the technology you're using, focusing on those that truly enhance your employees' ability to do their job.

Let's take a look at where technology can help your workplace productivity soar.

The Consequences of Poor Communication

Breakdowns in communication are one of the biggest threats to workplace productivity. According to a study presented by The Economist Intelligence Unit (EIU) and Lucidchart that examined the impact of poor connectivity and communication between coworkers, poor communication can cause stalled careers, a stressful and inefficient work environment, the inability to meet performance goals, and lost sales.* More specifically, the 403 junior staff, managers, and senior executives surveyed answered questions about how their work and their performance are impacted by the communication challenges they faced in the office. Their responses indicated that poor communication causes the following:

- Higher levels of stress (52 percent of participants)
- Projects that were delayed or considered failures (44 percent of participants)
- Lower morale (31 percent of participants)
- Missed or delayed performance goals (25 percent of participants)
- Lost sales (18 percent of participants)

Study respondents reported that of the sales lost, almost one-third of them had values between $100,000 and $999,999. And with almost one-fifth of the participants stating that poor communication had cost them sales, the potential cost to companies with inefficient connectivity systems is huge.

Lost sales are one threat posed by poor communication. Let's look at a few more figures regarding communication and the workplace. Poor collaboration can have a snowball effect that builds from a single frustrating encounter to a continually growing stress that has a significant impact upon the productivity of the office in general. This is not an isolated issue or one that is confined to a few specific industries. *Dynamic Signal*, in its "Annual State of Employee Communication and Engagement Study," found that as much as 80 percent of the workforce in the United States is stressed due to ineffective company communication.† Perhaps most notable about this information is that the number is rising despite the many communication solutions available. The 2019 report saw a 50 percent increase in stressed workers over 2018. The same report found that 70 percent of respondents felt overwhelmed as a direct result of fragmented communication.

---

*   Prnewswire.com. 2018. Miscommunications at Work Impact the Bottom Line, Study Finds. [online] Available at: <https://www.prnewswire.com/news-releases/miscommunications-at-work-impact-the-bottom-line-study-finds-300620637.html>.

†   2019. *2019 State of Employee Communication and Engagement Study.* [ebook] Available at: <https://resources.dynamicsignal.com/ebooks-guides/state-of-employee-communication-and-engagement-study-2019>.

Reinforcing these findings, research from the McKinsey Global Institute (MGI) found that high-skill and high-knowledge workers, including professionals and managers, saw their productivity increase by up to 25 percent after companies took the time to fully implement social technology solutions designed to keep employees in direct contact with each other.[*] The same report predicted that properly utilizing this kind of technology might translate to an increased annual revenue across four sectors—retail financial services, consumer packaged goods, professional services, and advanced manufacturing—of between $900 billion and $1.3 trillion.

These breakdowns in communication don't have to be massive to lead to reduced productivity and lost sales. They just have to exist prominently enough that the employee in question is unable to do their job to the best of their ability. This can stem from something as small as a missed email or a forgotten task by a single person. The important takeaways are that communication is extremely important to your bottom line and that it is vital to prevent even "small" communication breakdowns.

Data Struggles and Lost Time

Poor communication is not the only issue that can disrupt workplace productivity. Data management is another big concern. Your approach can either strengthen or undermine your communication system. If your employees need to fact-check specific figures or to review both current and past data for their projects, how easy is it for them to access that information? For many employees, the answer is "not very." That's a problem, because the more hurdles you put between an employee and the numbers they need, the longer it takes them to complete their tasks and meet their performance goals. And the longer it takes to complete their tasks, the lower their productivity and the higher the impact on your bottom line.

Related to the issue of poor communication, it's important to have a knowledge management system in place that enables employees to collaborate quickly and easily. But what happens when they're not sure whom to contact or how to reach employees with expertise on the subject at hand? Sometimes

*   Chui, M., Westergren, M., Sands, G., Sarrazin, H., Roxburgh, C., Dobbs, R., Bughin, J. and Manyika, J., 2012. The Social Economy: Unlocking Value and Productivity Through Social Technologies. [online] McKinsey Global Institute. Available at: <https://www.mckinsey.com/industries/technology-media-and-telecommunications/our-insights/the-social-economy>.

questions arise that require that information be exchanged between coworkers who rarely interact. In these situations, it can be difficult to determine exactly whom to reach out to for help. A knowledge management system maintains a database of individuals in the company, their roles, and their contact information. Making that list as easy as possible to access is one way of strengthening your company communication. After all, social technology solutions are only as good as the system that supports them. However, always put culture first. If you have a closed, stratified culture of "keep things to yourself," then knowledge management is a nonstarter. One of our government's greatest issues is that government agencies are not interconnected and don't share information. I see firms where managers don't share information. In fact, they hoard it. They don't allow employees to share information, and they restrict employees from doing so without their permission. In this stratified management system, productivity is strained, including larger issues such as employee engagement. Technology today provides the tools needed to share information freely within the organization. Your firm should encourage individuals to share information among peers and to situate white papers, reports, proposals, and wins in an easily searchable database. Train people how to build the database and how to use it.

Searching for information—whether about contacts within the company or data needed for a task—consumes a significant amount of time. In the previously referenced McKinsey Global Institute (MGI) report, researchers found that respondents spend almost 20 percent of their time at work tracking down internal information or searching for the right colleagues to help. Instead of being able to quickly find what they need and return to work, employees are forced to scour their limited social networks, rendering them unable to continue with their tasks until the proper data is located. Contributing to the problem is a lack of effective email management. MGI found that employees spend about 28 percent of their time at work sorting through emails. This time could be reduced if employees had the means to reach out directly to coworkers instead of sending email queries as well as via easy-to-use email management software that made it easy to sort, save, delete, and respond to email.

There are two different approaches here to consider. The first is how your data is organized and stored as well as the hoops through which your workers must jump in order to access it. Consider creating a streamlined process that enables employees to quickly search for what they need without having to contact multiple coworkers for help throughout the process. The second option is to create a strong internal communications system that makes it easy for employees to find and contact the person who might have the information they need.

These are not exclusive solutions. You should consider utilizing both options in order to make collaboration and data location as easy as possible. Why? In addition to reporting that workers spend approximately 20 percent of their time searching for information, MGI also found that implementing a searchable database along with effective communication solutions reduced the time spent searching by 35 percent. And when productivity is the factor in question, it is important to minimize the time spent away from actively contributing to the company.

Access to Tools and Data Can Improve Productivity

We know why it's important to strategically utilize technology to help improve communication and collaboration as well as to make data location and email management easier, but how exactly do you begin? For some, this step might seem particularly intimidating. But it's important to note that *not* providing your employees with the proper tools and information to help streamline their duties can cost you substantially. Failing to offer your employees this technology can leave you with productivity stats that must be optimized to significantly boost profits.

According to a study published in 2016 by *Ultimate Software*,[*] 92 percent of respondents reported that having access to technology that helped them efficiently complete their work was important. Almost one-third of those participants said that they would consider quitting their jobs if the technology were removed or outdated. Another report, published by CITO Research, found that 53 percent of respondents believed that mobile apps improved their productivity and streamlined business processes.[†] Recent research also

---

[*]   Ultimate Software. 2016. Ultimate Software—New National Study Uncovers Notable Shift in Factors Influencing Employee Job Satisfaction, Engagement. [online] Available at: <https://www.ultimatesoftware.com/PR/Press-Release/New-National-Study-Uncovers-Notable-Shift-in-Factors-Influencing-Employee-Job-Satisfaction-Engagement>.

[†]   2016. *2016 Executive Enterprise Mobility Report*. [ebook] Available at: <https://go.appe rian.com/rs/300-EOJ-215/images/Apperian%202016%20Executive%20Enterprise%20 Mobility%20Report_FINAL_20160216.pdf?aliId=16373787>.

found that establishing a unified communications (UC) system not only saw workplace productivity rise by 52 percent but also resulted in an operating profit increase of 25 percent.*

Are you ready to consider implementing technology such as data management apps, email management apps, and communication apps in your workplace? It isn't nearly as difficult as it sounds. First, consider that your employees likely want to complete their work more easily than they currently are. If you take your time and select only the technology that you truly need, they shouldn't be too overwhelmed with the changes, minimizing the amount of downtime you might experience as they learn to operate their new tools. Remember: Keep it simple. As an example, an independent survey carried out by harmon.ie found that 67 percent of respondents thought that focusing on work would be easier if their apps fit in a single window. This highlights the importance of keeping the number of apps themselves to a minimum.†

There are many technological options available to you. If your employees tend to be out of the office frequently, then you might consider wearable options. From smart glasses to smart watches and beyond, the smart application of technology is possible even for employees who spend most of their time in the field or in a warehouse.‡ And for those who spend their time mostly behind their desk, the options are even more abundant. Take time to look into a solid social platform that enables your employees to communicate and collaborate easily. Consider which tools they need to work more efficiently, and don't hesitate to ask them for their opinions. Reaching out to your workforce is a great way to gain insight into their process, enabling you to find the best tools possible for their needs. And don't forget to also invest in solid email and data management software. Keep your goal—to make it easier for your employees to focus on and complete their work—in mind as you weigh your options.

---

* McCarver, M., n.d. How Unified Communications Boosts Workplace Productivity. [online] Sangoma. Available at: <https://www.sangoma.com/articles/workplace-productivity/?utm_source=digium_redirect>.

† Businesswire.com. 2017. Information and App Overload Hurts Worker Productivity, Focus and Morale Worldwide, According to New Independent Survey. [online] Available at: <https://www.businesswire.com/news/home/20170918005033/en/Information-App-Overload-Hurts-Worker-Productivity-Focus>.

‡ Miller, J., 2020. Wearable Tech Is Increasing Worker Productivity, Safety and Performance. [online] Technology Solutions That Drive Business. Available at: <https://biztechmagazine.com/article/2020/02/wearable-tech-increasing-worker-productivity-safety-and-performance>.

Along with this information, and these precautions, here is another aspect regarding technology. Smart solutions can improve productivity, but modern technology can also work to boost employee wellness both in and out of the office. An abundance of options exists, from wearable technology to apps that install on phones or computers, to motivate employees to engage with each other and to help them meet their wellness goals.

I've already discussed why wellness, in all aspects of the word, is important to employee success and productivity. However, I haven't spent much time explaining how to motivate employees to take advantage of the resources you are providing to them. Many employees will take initiative on their own and actively seek out resources to boost their health and sense of well-being, but others will need help getting started. That's where technology comes in. Be aware, however, that this can be a double-edged sword; you might have to set guidelines as to when and where apps and standalone products can be used. It doesn't do much good to limit the number of productivity apps in the workplace if they're replaced by other distractions. So consider these options carefully and make the choices that are a good fit for your goals, your workforce, and your organization's culture. And don't forget that these tips are also tailored to your own potential needs. I'm offering them from an employer-to-employee perspective, but everything here is applicable to your own life and routine as well.

Wearable Trackers

Wearable trackers are one form of technology that can encourage workers to engage with wellness initiatives. There is a wide array of options in this category. From watches to bracelets to anklets and just about everything in between, there is usually a wearable style to fit any taste. The technology works by tracking physical activity during the day, including steps walked, stairs climbed, and the number of calories burned given the aforementioned activities. You can do various things with this kind of technology too. One option might be to start an interoffice competition designed to measure progress among all entrants. The individual who wins might be awarded something minor or simply have bragging rights—the choice is yours. You can also allow employees to use the devices without any kind of external motivation such as a contest. Many will likely appreciate the ability to quietly keep track of their wellness without input from anyone else.

Games and Contests

This is worth a more detailed look. Humans are competitive by nature, and achieving goals is something that is hardwired into our psyche, especially if doing so gives us the opportunity to get ahead in some way. This is one reason why creating contests and "gamifying" the wellness process can be an extremely effective engagement tool. Whether the employee's objective is to achieve specific fitness aims, to eat more healthfully, or to lose weight, making the process fun is often the best way to motivate your workers to stick to their goals and succeed, thereby improving the overall wellness of the workforce in general.

Apps

Mobile applications are another wellness-related technological option to consider. These can be used alone or in conjunction with wearable trackers to help employees monitor their progress and to encourage them along the way. Some apps can even measure things such as sleeping habits, better enabling your employees to identify potential health issues or sleeping issues that might be standing in the way of productivity and overall wellness. Some apps are designed specifically to track and improve mental health, which wearable trackers and contests can't achieve. Making use of these is a great way to encourage employees to pay attention to all aspects of their health.

Is technology right for your workplace wellness initiatives? It doesn't have to be. If you don't see the value in the points I've raised, your wellness programs will likely still function just fine. But if you're hoping to optimize engagement and results, investing in modern solutions can make achieving and maintaining wellness a fun process rather than one that feels thankless and drawn out.

What is the bottom line here? The importance of technology in many aspects of the workplace cannot be overstated, but neither can its potential pitfalls. In order to assess the best fit for your business and ensure that the options available to your employees improve productivity rather than distract them, you must take some time to explore how your workforce currently operates. Look at what your employees are doing and consider whether or not technology can improve the process.

On a more personal level, ensure that you make *your health* and your productivity priorities. Encouraging your employees to do better is important, but ensuring that you are leading by example is equally important. Consider how technology can improve your days. And think about the guidelines, advice, and tips I've given as you look at various options. Don't be afraid to experiment. Finding the right technology combination can significantly improve your daily productivity and effectiveness, so don't shy away from the initial time investment.

Technology can be excellent for your organization and your productivity. It just takes some consideration to find the right options. Keep your own efficiency in mind as you recommend certain applications or implement technological enhancements for your workforce.

Now is the time to reassess your workforce. Reevaluate their needs and take a look at your current systems with critical eyes. Finding the right combination of technology can help significantly improve workplace productivity and your bottom line.

The Business Case

Consider this example of the benefits of improving technology in your company:

As mentioned earlier, the MGI report found that respondents spent almost 20 percent of their time at work tracking down internal information or searching for the right colleagues for help or internal collaboration. This corresponds to one entire day out of a five-day workweek. MGI research also estimates that the use of collaboration technologies (using this one strategy as an example) can increase workers' productivity by 25 to 35 percent.[*]

Part A (cost of no change):

Given the 20 percent estimate of wasted time:

    a. 1,000 employees.

    b. 20 percent of time lost = 52 days out of 260 workdays.

    c. $75,000 average salary x 20 percent.

    d. $15,000 per employee x 1,000 employees = $15,000,000 of lost time.

---

[*]   Chui, M., Westergren, M., Sands, G., Sarrazin, H., Roxburgh, C., Dobbs, R., Bughin, J. and Manyika, J., 2012. The Social Economy: Unlocking Value and Productivity Through Social Technologies. [online] McKinsey Global Institute. Available at: <https://www.mckinsey.com/industries/technology-media-and-telecommunications/our-insights/the-social-economy>.

Part B (gain by implementing collaborative technologies):

Assume that the cost of implementing collaboration technologies is $100,000. The implementation of such technology would increase productivity by 25 to 35 percent, as previously mentioned. This means that the technology would free up at least 25 percent of employees' paid time. The average annual value of that time is 25 percent x $75,000 = $18,750 per employee. This equals a total annual gain for the employer of $18,750,000.

For further reading about technology, see Appendix E.

CHAPTER SEVEN
Key Component #5— Optimizing Your Workday (Getting 30 Hours Out of 24)

CEO: Today's topic is exciting for me because it's about us as individuals, not as a group—how we each can improve on our own. Anybody have any ideas on how to get started?

Milton: Shall we get started by speaking about our daily tasks, even from getting up in the morning?

CEO: I think that's a terrific idea. Let's start right from the beginning. What do you do when you get up in the morning? What's the first thing you do?

Bethany: You mean as soon as I get out of bed?

Kent: Yes.

Milton: I check my email right away then I go straight to the bathroom.

CEO: Okay, would it be more efficient to change that?

Kent: Cut out checking my email as soon as I roll over.

CEO: I believe that will be more productive. Studies show that you should only check emails twice a day to be most productive. I don't think in today's environment that is acceptable, but why not? What if I set the culture to do so? What if I asked all my managers to change, not to expect employees to look at their emails so often—don't expect a quick reply—and don't encourage one?

Bethany: Wow, imagine that.

CEO: I can do it, you know. I am the CEO. Shall I?

Bethany, Kent, Milton: Yes!

CEO: But will it improve our lives?

Kent: For sure.

CEO: Why?

Kent: Because it would reduce my stress level.

CEO: Okay, anything else?

Kent: And it will make me more productive because with stress there are ancillary effects; health problems which leads to absenteeism, non-engagement, and mistakes at work.

CEO: Wow, that's terrific. Do we all agree?

(They all nod.)

CEO: Well then, there's our answer. I'll get the management team together and announce the new initiative. No checking emails more than twice a day.

The final component we're going to explore might just be the most important. Everything discussed in earlier chapters is vital to creating a healthy organization ready to flourish and grow, but it all hinges on your ability to put in the work necessary to make changes and boost your productivity in the workplace. If you aren't able to focus on the task at hand and steadily work toward your goal, how can you expect your employees to follow your lead?

The truth is that your organization's success depends on your personal success—your personal dedication and productivity. That's why this chapter is a "personal optimization" chapter dedicated to ensuring that your time at work is as productive as possible. Don't dismiss it based on the assumption that you're already doing well. There's always room for improvement, and you might be surprised at what best practices dictate for optimal workplace productivity versus how you're currently structuring your days.

Let's take a look at what impacts your workday and how you can adapt your routine to ensure your focus is always exactly where it needs to be. Let's see how you can get 30 hours out of your day. There is no way, of course, to expand time, right? Wrong. There is a way to expand your own time. Take the assumption in the illustration below that your day is split into thirds. There is one third of your day that you have very little control over and that's sleep. For illustrative purposes I assumed eight hours of sleep. If you get less, then this only gives you more time for work and play. What I'm suggesting is that you can expand your time of work and play an additional six hours to get more out of your life. Time is actually relative. We know that the further you're away from Gravity time expands. We also know that the slower you

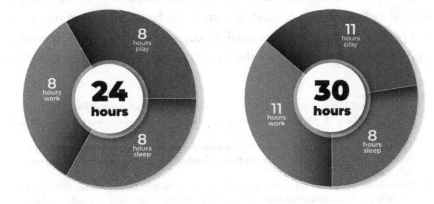

move time expands. There is scientific proof that time isn't absolute. As you follow along, maybe you'll agree that you can actually get the equivalent of 30 hours out of the day.

What Impacts Your Workday?

For most people, the workday consists of several different tasks. Many of these are universal and apply to almost all industries, including things like managing email, returning phone calls, and inputting information into a mobile device, a PC, or both. And this isn't idle work that is quickly accomplished. In fact, responding to email alone can soak up far more time than it should.

According to a study conducted by Adobe exploring email use in both the professional and personal spheres, most American workers spend five hours or more checking email daily.* This time is split into two categories—work email and personal email. On average, workers reported spending 209 minutes on work email and 143 minutes on personal email. Together, they spent about 352 minutes total on their in-box every day. That means that during the average workday, assuming attention is focused solely on work, people spend more than three hours on email alone.

That number might be less surprising when you consider that most businesspeople reported receiving 122 emails every day, but it's no less concerning.† Three hours is quite a bit of time to spend on any task, much less emails that are likely less important than other projects. Note that this doesn't account for the amount of time it takes to refocus after being distracted. According to an interview with a professor from the University of California's Department of Informatics, today's workers take just over 23 minutes to get back on task after they've switched gears from checking email to returning to a project.‡ If you check your email throughout the day—in other words, you're not spending only those three hours in the in-box—you're spending

---

* Hess, A., 2019. Here's How Many Hours American Workers Spend on Email Each Day. [online] CNBC. Available at: <https://www.cnbc.com/2019/09/22/heres-how-many-hours-american-workers-spend-on-email-each-day.html>.

† Lam, B., 2016. Bosses Don't Want Overwhelmed Employees Either. [online] *The Atlantic.* Available at: <https://www.theatlantic.com/business/archive/2016/03/too-many-emails/471918/>.

‡ Pattison, K., 2008. Worker, Interrupted: The Cost of Task Switching. [online] *Fast Company.* Available at: <https://www.fastcompany.com/944128/worker-interrupted-cost-of-task-switching>.

23 minutes after every visit attempting to refocus and give your other tasks your undivided attention. How many times a day do you "quickly" take a peek at your email while working on other things?

This is only one example of how a poorly structured day can significantly impact your ability to give your job the attention it deserves, and we haven't even talked about multitasking yet. When your workday is structured properly and you implement strategies to improve your productivity and focus, your performance will increase along with the quality of your work.

I have some advice and tips I'd like to share that help make my workday a productive one.

Walkersize

One of the best things you can do to boost your focus and productivity at work is to take a walk. I do so every morning and will get 5,000 steps in before breakfast. The rest is on a treadmill desk which I mentioned earlier. According to a study by the American Psychological Association, taking even a short walk outside and then returning to the office significantly boosted participants' creative thinking ability.[*] More specifically, 81 percent of the individuals studied were found to have increased creative divergent thinking after their walks. This means that they were better able to formulate new ideas and find smart solutions to the problems they might be facing with a task or project.

It's not just creativity that exercise, including walking, has shown to increase, either. Cognitive function in general and time management in particular have also been tied to exercise, with individuals committed to spending even 10 minutes on physical activity a few times a day experiencing measurable benefits. Exercising is also a good way to improve your energy levels, especially if you tend to experience a "slump" in the afternoon.[†]

If you aren't able to head outside for a brisk walk during the workday, that's okay. Walking on a treadmill inside was also shown to help. One of the

---

[*]   Oppezzo, M. and Schwartz, D., 2014. Give Your Ideas Some Legs: The Positive Effect of Walking on Creative Thinking. *Journal of Experimental Psychology: Learning, Memory, and Cognition*, 40(4): 1142–1152.

[†]   Tate, C., 2015. 6 Reasons Why Exercise Can Supercharge Your Productivity. [online] The Next Web. Available at: <https://thenextweb.com/lifehacks/2015/07/12/6-reasons-why-exercise-can -supercharge-your-productivity/#.tnw_qioEUREs>.

easiest ways to accommodate this tip is via the use of a treadmill desk. You don't have to use it all day long. As previously mentioned, even a few times a day can offer a big payoff in terms of focus and brain function. It can also improve your overall health and well-being, the importance of which we've covered in previous chapters. Why not increase your physical activity while also boosting your creative thinking?

If a treadmill desk sounds like a bit more than you'd like to tackle, consider a standing desk instead. Sitting in front of your computer all day isn't the best way to remain engaged with your work, nor is it good for your overall productivity. A standing desk, on the other hand, gives you the opportunity to stretch your legs as you check email and keep your body moving, even if only by a small amount.

Focus, Don't Multitask

Here's the truth about multitasking: it doesn't work. Any neuroscientist will tell you that. I touched on this briefly in an earlier chapter, but it's important enough to bear repeating. Many people believe they're "great" multitaskers—that they can effortlessly switch between tasks and projects with minimal loss of focus. But what about those 23 minutes we talked about above? If you're constantly switching between tasks, you're never truly focused on any of them, because it takes 23 minutes just to get back on track every time you shift gears.

Even more than the time it takes to focus after changing tasks, however, is the fact that multitasking isn't humanly possible. Or, to be slightly more accurate, it's just not something our brains are capable of doing well. That means that you might technically be able to carry on a phone conversation while typing an email, but neither activity will be completed as efficiently and quickly as it would if you weren't attempting to multitask.[*]

Multitasking doesn't make you any more productive, either. How could it? We now know that it takes our brains about 23 minutes to refocus on a task. If you're attempting to complete two or more tasks at once, you're not giving your mind enough time to focus on any of them. Additionally, your chance of making errors increases. One study found that attempting to multitask while tasked with buying specific items led to consumers making the

---

[*]   Korkki, P., n.d. *How To Make The Most Of Your Workday*. [online] Nytimes.com. Available at: <https://www.nytimes.com/guides/business/how-to-improve-your-productivity-at-work>.

wrong choices much more often than those who weren't multitasking.* What does this mean for today's professional? Multitasking takes your attention away from small details. You might be able to accurately complete a task but are more likely to make small errors throughout it, lowering the project's overall quality.

Instead of multitasking, stick with something until you complete it. That means that instead of talking to a client on the phone while working on another project, pick one or the other. You'll make better choices in the conversation—and recall the information you're given easier—if that's all you're doing. And the project will benefit from an attention span that isn't split between two different activities.

If you aren't quite sure how to stop multitasking and still have time to complete everything you need to finish, don't worry—we're tackling that problem next.

Schedule Priorities

There's an important question you should ask yourself every night: "What's important tomorrow?"

In order to maximize your productivity and focus, you must be able to discern between what is important and what is urgent. Though these might sound the same, there is a significant difference between them. Important tasks are tasks that absolutely must be completed or progressed—they are vital to a project or a deal, and not finishing them on time would be disastrous. Things that are urgent might require a response as quickly as possible, but they won't have a long-term impact. An email might be urgent, for example, if an employee or a client has a question but if the response takes a bit longer than they'd like, the world won't end. If you fail to complete an important report or proposal, on the other hand, you could be setting your department back in terms of progress and even hold up other important projects that depend on your work.

The above example might not fit your job precisely, but the meaning is universal. Instead of focusing on things that are urgent, focus first on things that are important. Once you have the latter squared away, you will have

---

* Selin Atalay, A., Onur Bodur, H. and Bressoud, E., 2017. When and How Multitasking Impacts Consumer Shopping Decisions. *Journal of Retailing*, 93(2): 187–200.

more time and energy to devote to the former. Consider creating a list every night of important tasks that must be completed by the end of the next business day. Once you have them listed, pick the most important and begin your day with that task. Ideally, this would happen before checking and responding to emails.

If you must check email before you get started on your important tasks, that's okay, but schedule time to check your in-box and reply (remember, to be fully productive, you should only check emails twice a day—good luck with that, right?). If you know you have to check your email in the morning, schedule half an hour or an hour devoted strictly to managing your in-box. If you know you'll have more to answer throughout the day, consider scheduling another block or two of time for the task, too. The point is to get through your email as quickly as possible so that you have the time to focus on the important things.

In addition to scheduling your emails so that you aren't tempted to check in throughout the day and throw your productivity off, try to spend as little time as possible on the things that aren't important. That doesn't mean to rush through them, of course—complete them just as you would any other task. But don't dwell on them. Something that isn't overly important in the long haul doesn't necessarily need as much of your time and attention as something that has immediate and long-term impact.

Make time for your priorities. Find a way that you will not be disturbed.

Structure Your Day

You now know that it's beneficial to have important tasks mapped out before the day begins, but the amount of time you devote to each task is just as essential. Our minds were not made to focus on something deeply for hours and hours. In fact, most of us begin to lose steam after about 90 minutes. Consider building your day in 90-minute segments followed by 20- to 30-minute breaks. Take advantage of the downtime by hitting the treadmill or heading outside for a quick walk to refresh your body and mind.

If you know a task won't take 90 minutes of time, combine it with something else. While it's not good to switch between tasks constantly, moving from task to task as you complete is only logical. Perhaps you know answering emails will take about half an hour and returning client phone calls will take around an hour, for example. These two tasks naturally work together to fill up a 90-minute block.

Focus less on completing a task in 90 minutes and more on simply staying focused and working for the block of time, even if that means only partially completing something before you take a quick break. The time off will give you even better focus when you return.

The goal in structuring your day is to take ownership of it. Building your day around the tasks you deem important gives you the opportunity to take action yourself rather than simply react to the things around you. Sometimes these distractions simply can't be helped, and sometimes urgent tasks are also emergencies that cannot be delayed. Do your best to stick to your schedule as much as possible—you'll be more productive for the effort.

Getting through the workday doesn't have to be difficult. Taking even just a few minutes every afternoon or night to think about what needs to be accomplished the next day and blocking out specific chunks of time for each task will help you flow seamlessly into them. Plus, it may help you sleep better.

Finally, here's me at my desk:

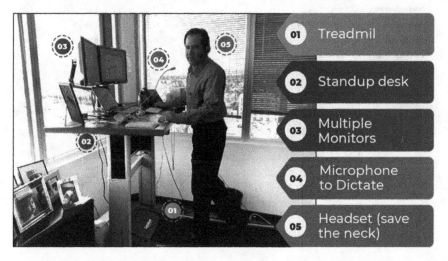

01	Treadmil
02	Standup desk
03	Multiple Monitors
04	Microphone to Dictate
05	Headset (save the neck)

It's not just a stand-up desk. It's a treadmill desk. Multiple monitors. A microphone to dictate. A headset to save any neck pain and I'm exercising while I'm doing my work. While I'm not a proponent of multitasking, you can actually walk 1.3 miles per hour unconsciously and still be working, even talking. In fact, I'm writing this book on my treadmill desk exactly like the image above.

The Business Case

I have calculated the benefits of optimizing your workday. Below is the business case if all employees optimized their workday. You can see in a professional services company of 1,000 employees the benefit to top-line revenue is significant: **$261,000,000**.

Description	Evidence Based Assumptions	Time Saved (min)	Increased Productivity (min)	Rate/min ($)	Increased Productivity ($)
Breakfast	Stabilize and energy	30	30	3.33	$100
Exercise	Stabilize and energy	30	30	3.33	$100
Transcription service for vm's	20 vm's/day	30 seconds/vm	10	3.33	$33
Dictate Emails	30 vm's/day	1 min/email x 35	35	3.33	$117
Keyboard Shortcuts	15 min/day	15	15	3.33	$50
Optimize Task List	30 min/day	30	30	3.33	$100
Use a Password Manager	10 min/day	10	10	3.33	$33
Improve typing speed	15 min/day	15	15	3.33	$50
Avoid Distractions	30 min/day	30	30	3.33	$100
Manage email	10 distractions x	50	50	3.33	$167
Avoid multitasking	Focus	30	30	3.33	$100
Get enough sleep	Focus/productivity	30	30	3.33	$100
Increase monitor size	26" monitor	30	30	3.33	$100
Add another monitor	Two 19" monitors	69	60	3.33	$200
Nap for 10 minutes	10 min/day	30	30	3.33	$100
		Total minutes =	435	Daily increase	$1,450
		minutes = 1 hr	60	work days/yr	240
		Hours	7.25	Annual incr/person	$348,000
				employees	1000
			Assumed % efficiency gained		75%
				Total	$261,000,000

For further reading about optimizing your workday, see Appendix F.

CHAPTER EIGHT
Adapting to Change

CEO: Our sessions are almost at an end—only one more after this. I greatly appreciate everybody's time out of their busy days to meet with me to help the firm improve its performance through productivity— excuse me—compassionate productivity. To remind everyone, I refer to compassionate productivity as a sensitive means to get the most out of our days. This includes our personal lives. While I'm the CEO of the firm and my job is to improve performance, I'm an individual just like the rest of you, with my family, friends, and relationships that I want to continue to develop and nurture. So it's important to me, and I believe this in my heart, there is a way to improve performance/productivity in the firm and to do so in your own lives. Productivity can cross both borders: work and home. Today, let's talk about adapting to change. Anybody have any ideas how we should start?

Bethany: First, I want to thank you for reaching out to us over this time to discuss the company and how to improve it. I can't speak for the others but for me, that in itself, has improved my engagement in my job. Knowing how interested you are in our lives makes me want to do my work better.

Milton: I agree. Thank you.

Kent: Me too.

CEO: Thank you. Now, let's address adapting to change. You'll find there are a lot of tips. If you can adapt to three of these, you'll make a great leap. There is a saying, "How do you eat an elephant?" Answer: "One bite at a time."

What's the first thing you should do when you get up in the morning? Do something different and you're already on your way to a more productive day. I don't mean do something different every day. But if it's as small as changing the pocket you put money in, or rearranging your cash in a new way, it will jog your brain. When your brain gets jogged, it gets stimulated. When it gets stimulated, it becomes more productive.

Now that we've talked about the five components essential to increasing your productivity as well as streamlining your business operations, it's time to examine a few additional points as we move toward the end of the book. I've talked about the importance of being flexible and willing to change your daily routine in order to adopt a schedule that promotes productivity rather than inhibits it, but we haven't delved into the details yet.

There are many factors that can impact your day. Some of the big ones were discussed in earlier chapters, but that still leaves quite a bit of ground to cover. In this chapter, I want to look at the often-overlooked changes you can make to even further optimize your time in the office.

Implement a Voicemail Transcription Service

If you receive a lot of calls, it's inevitable that you miss at least a few every day. And while it might not seem like much time in the moment, dedicating a few moments to pulling up your voicemail, listening to the message, and taking note of the pertinent information can really add up over the course of a day, much less a workweek. This is one of the reasons voicemail transcription services are worth a look.

Voicemail transcription services, as the name implies, transcribe voicemails and send them to you via SMS or email. This is most conveniently and quickly done via an automated process that can have your voicemail transcribed and sent to you in text form almost immediately after it is left. This saves you the trouble of navigating through your voicemail message system, something that can take a bit of time if you're using proper security methods like PINs or computer prompts. With a voicemail transcription service, there's no need to worry about any of that.

Avoiding your voicemail system isn't the only reason to consider investing in a transcription service, of course. Have you ever found yourself searching your mind for information from a client you believe was included in a voicemail you received a week or three back? When that happens, you only have a few options. You can sift through your voicemail system and listen to each and every message until you find the right one or, if your voicemails are deleted automatically, you can admit defeat and ask your client to send the details again. Frankly, neither is a great solution. When your voicemails are transcribed, it's easy to set up a searchable database in your in-box. That means that you can quickly search your messages with a simple query or filter, making finding the right information painless.

Dictate Your Emails

If you've ever attempted to return an email or text while running errands or driving from one office to another, you've probably realized just how difficult juggling different tasks can be. Not only is it not safe to focus on your phone instead of the road, but it's not particularly efficient, either. Perhaps you've simply found that sitting down and spending half an hour typing emails is somewhat tedious and leaves your mind a bit hazy. Whatever the reason, the truth is that emails can impact your productivity in a big way. It can take a lot of time to answer them, especially if you're not a particularly proficient typist, and so much downtime can leave your mind struggling to focus.

The solution is dictating your emails. Instead of worrying about replying on the go or spending time in your office typing away at your keyboard, consider using a dictation app to help the process along. You can quickly reply verbally, and the app will record your message as text—it's quick and easy. Don't worry about messy emails with wrong words or missing punctuation, either. Today's voice-to-text software is far more accurate than it was in the past, offering intuitive transcription options. And when you're speaking rather than typing, you'll find that not only is responding to emails quicker, but it's much more mentally engaging, too. That means you can get right back to work once you're done going through your in-box with little downtime needed to refocus yourself.

Use Keyboard Shortcuts

If you're not using keyboard shortcuts, you might be wasting quite a bit of time. We explored why talking is preferable to typing above, but there are some times we must be on our keyboards. When we do, we want that time to be as productive as possible. Let me give you an example of just how quick and easy keyboard shortcuts can be. Have you ever used "Ctrl+A" to select text, "Ctrl+C" to copy it, and "Ctrl+V" to paste it? Those are all keyboard shortcuts, and they save quite a bit of time. Try manually selecting all of your text and then copying and pasting it using your application's menu—it will take noticeably more time. And even a few seconds can quickly add up.

The bottom line here is that keyboard shortcuts are time-saving and efficient, giving you the opportunity to zip through your tasks without spending unnecessary time on your keyboard. From accessing the dictionary while writing to quickly inserting boxes and images, shortcuts make work easier.

Optimize Your Task List

Spending more time than you need to work only lowers your overall productivity in the long run and means potentially running out of time to meet important due dates. As we explored in an earlier chapter, a task list is a vital component of an organized day. Creating and using that list properly, however, can be a bit trickier.

There are several professionals who speak to this topic well, and I've read many books on how to manage my task list. There are many approaches and they are all good. I follow Michael Linenberger's *One Minute To-Do List* and it works really well for me. He suggests breaking out your list in Critical Now, Opportunity Now, and Over the Horizon sections. It takes a load of stress off my day because I always feel like I've accomplished what I've intended to do. There are others who have their own system. Find one and live by it.

At the very least, create the list the day before you need it and review it first thing in the morning. Take a look at the tasks you need to accomplish and consider how much time you'll likely need to spend on each. If there's a task you particularly dislike—or one that makes you anxious—get it done as soon as possible. Putting it off only means that the back of your mind is tied up worrying about it rather than focusing on the task at hand. Getting it out of the way prevents that from happening and also gives you a boost of relief you can channel into your next projects.

Finally, you might consider organizing your list by blocks of time. The idea is that you work as hard as possible during that block and then you take a break after you're done. That last part is vital—your mind will need the rest after the time you've spent powering through work, so make sure to include downtime at the end of each block (or between them).

Using a Password Manager

In a world where internet security is absolutely vital, who has time to remember all of their passwords? Because each one should be completely different from any other and contain all manner of symbols and numbers, it quickly becomes impossible to memorize each and every one. Equally time-consuming is writing passwords down and referring to the list every time you need to login somewhere. Not only is the list a potential security hazard, but it takes time to find it, consult it, and type the password properly.

The better solution is to use a password manager. This kind of application records your login information to different sites and automatically inputs them into the login fields when you visit a website. All you have to do is click "login" and go about your business without the need to look up any password or user-name at all. Make sure to select a well-established option that encrypts your password lists so that if a data breach occurs, your information will be safe.

Improving Your Typing Speed

This isn't something that everyone considers, but your typing speed has a huge impact on how quickly you can complete projects. If you aren't an adept typist and have to watch your fingers as you input every keystroke, for example, it might take you easily three times as long to finish your work than it would someone who is able to type "blind." This isn't productive at all. It's a poor use of your time and causes you to spend far more time on your work than needed.

The prospect of improving your typing speed might not be an immediately appealing one, but it's one of the best things you can do to improve the amount of work you can complete in a single day. There are numerous apps and practices online that can help you accomplish this goal—and note that you don't have to be an incredible typist. It's enough to simply be competent and type faster than you do right now.

Avoid Distractions and Focus

Working in an office can be difficult sometimes. From sharing common spaces to finding coworkers popping into your office every ten minutes, it can be incredibly difficult to sit down and truly focus on your work. As a result, you'll spend more time refocusing and attempting to complete tasks than you will be completely engaged with your work.

The answer here is both easy and hard to implement: close your door. Take some time to explain to your coworkers why you're doing this if your workplace has a culture of quick chats throughout the day and closing your door might be seen as rude. The intent here is not to hurt feelings, but rather to give you the time to focus on what is most important—completing your work quickly and efficiently. Once you've explained why you might close your door, go ahead and shut it and dive into your projects! You might even consider posting a note on the door itself explaining that you're in the middle of something and should only be disturbed for emergencies to dissuade anyone who might be tempted to knock.

Manage Email

Email has been a recurring point of discussion in this book, and for good reason. It can quickly consume a significant chunk of your time at work every day, leaving you with less time to work on important projects. In order to avoid spending too much time on this task, I have two simple pieces of advice: turn off notifications and zero out your in-box every day.

The goal here is to make email something that you check at specific times of the day, not something that interrupts your work. Turning off notifications ensures that you won't be interrupted in the middle of something every time an email hits your in-box. You don't have to answer every email the second you receive it—a turnaround time of 24 hours is usually completely acceptable, especially if it means that you're boosting your productivity elsewhere.

In addition, make it a goal to keep your in-box at "zero" as much as possible. Don't read a message and put off the reply by marking it "unread" and allowing it to sit there. You'll be thinking about the need to respond before you leave the office while attempting to work on other things. Even beyond that, answering everything in your in-box in one fell swoop allows you to tie up any loose strings and truly focus on other things.

Avoid Multitasking

We've explored this issue in detail in earlier chapters, but it's worth noting again: don't attempt to multitask. It's not something our brains can do, and it splits your focus between the activities in question, ensuring that neither is receiving your full attention. It ultimately will take you longer to complete lower-quality work than you would if you simply focused on each task individually.

Get Enough Sleep

This piece of advice can be tricky to implement, but it's absolutely imperative to your day. You must get enough sleep. The exact number of hours can vary from person to person, but it typically is about six to seven hours for adults. Whatever your ideal duration, make sure to consistently hit that time. Getting enough sleep helps our brains and bodies alike recover from daily stresses and refresh themselves for upcoming tasks. If you get too little sleep and feel as though you're dragging your way through the day reliant on mugs of coffee, your attention and focus will suffer along with the speed and quality of your work.

If you want to optimize your time in the office and reach your maximum productivity level, sleep is essential. If that means shifting a nonessential task to another day, then so be it.

Nap for 10 Minutes a Day

You might be surprised to find napping on the list of tips to improve productivity, but research shows that a quick nap can immediately improve cognitive function, with benefits lasting for as long as 155 minutes.* The most effective nap length was found to be 10 minutes. Any less than that and the nap produces little improvement and any longer delays the benefits to cognitive performance. Additionally, naps of 30 minutes or longer led to sleep inertia, the feeling of grogginess that can hit after waking up. Ten minutes is the sweet spot, and the time spent results in multiple benefits that will significantly boost your performance for the rest of the day.

Keep in mind that napping can interfere with your nighttime sleep if you wait too long in the day. The early afternoon and late morning are the best times of the day to nap.

---

* DiSalvo, D., 2012. Why You Should Take a 10-Minute Nap Every Day. [online] *Forbes*. Available at: <https://www.forbes.com/sites/daviddisalvo/2012/07/24/why-you-should-take-a-10-minute-nap-every-day/#524759751b0f>.

The advice in this chapter might seem like a lot to take in, and that's okay—you don't have to change the entirety of your daily routine at once. Focus on implementing three of these tips right away. Do more as you get accustomed to them and soon they become second nature. Being able to adapt your routine will boost your productivity and make it easier to perform better at work.

For further reading about adapting to change, see Appendix G.

CHAPTER NINE
The Next 24 Hours

CEO: There is an expression, "Task management is a management issue." Do you believe that?

Bethany: Not exactly clear on what that means.

CEO: It means managing your tasks at work is really the responsibility of your manager.

Milton: I believe that's true to a certain extent, but isn't it also true that responsibility rests with managers and direct reports?

CEO: I agree. I think it's important that we empower employees to succeed. The more the employee feels empowered, the better results and the more productive the employee will become. Now that we're entering the next 24 hours and we've concluded our sessions, I'd like to start implementing some of these initiatives. Your thoughts?

Bethany: I'm all in.

(The others also agree and smile.)

CEO: Thank you for attending these coffee klatches. You made a great difference in my life, and I hope I'm able to do the same in yours. Just one more question. I'm creating the position of Director of Productivity. Do you know anyone who may want that position?

(They all emphatically raise their hands.)

The next 24 hours are crucial. You're done reading this book, and, like many of us do after finishing a book, we simply move on. That would be a big mistake here. You may feel like you'll get to some of these initiatives at one point or another, but if you procrastinate, you're not likely to come back to them. The initiatives in this book take hard work. Yes, I said hard work. And in order to do that you have to work smart. If you work smart and implement these initiatives, the rewards will be a higher stock price, more success for the firm, and happier, engaged employees.

The tools in this book are designed to work in totality. If you want your firm to grow, prosper, and have a legacy that you built, each of the productivity improvements in this book needs to be initiated. While the tools need to come in at a pace the organization can handle, they are designed to work as a whole. You've likely been pitched how important an engagement survey or a wellness campaign is to conduct, but if it is not done in concert with a total strategy of productivity advances with a clear timetable and a one- to two-year plan on implementing these tools, then you're doing it halfway. Take the bull by the horns and make change in your organization. Don't wait for a catastrophe, a recession, or another excuse. Take the initiative and implement productivity measures that will improve results and improve lives of the individuals who work for you. Be a leader.

We've talked about quite a bit in this book. From recognizing the important foundations of a healthy personal and business life to implementing steps to optimize your productivity as well as that of your employees, the information covered has been comprehensive and detailed. You might even feel as though you know enough now to reshape your business and your own habits to promote happiness and efficiency alike. One point to remember, however, is that there are a few decisions you must make in order to effect strong, lasting change.

Collect Data and Make a Plan to Change

Information is important, but also ultimately useless unless it is used. That means that understanding the facts and advice you've read here and half-heartedly following some of them is not enough. That information must be applied systematically in every facet of your life in order to truly revolutionize your workday.

In this chapter, we're going to look at how you can spend the next 24 hours in the most productive way possible and use the knowledge you've acquired to make a plan for change. Nothing will change until you take concrete actions to push yourself and your business forward—having a detailed plan is vital to successfully building a healthier and more productive organization and personal routine while encouraging your employees to live more balanced and productive lives, too. Remember that when everyone is on the same page and works to achieve the same goal, everything flows much more quickly and smoothly.

Your goal for the next 24 hours, then, is to create a comprehensive plan to measure where you are currently and where you and your employees can improve, complete with an action plan and due dates.

Understanding the Baseline

The baseline is where you begin. This might not be anywhere near where you want to eventually be, but that's okay—this is the starting point, not the finish line. Don't spend too much time dwelling on the less-than-perfect, in other words, and focus instead on where and how to improve your situation. This will be the measure against which you will examine future progress.

In order to fully understand your baseline, you will need to do a few different things to measure and establish your current situation.

Measurement Methods

Quantifying your business operations can help you find trends and patterns you might otherwise miss while also giving you information about how a particular goal or change is impacting various parts of the business. Not all metrics are the same, however, and it is important to understand what method of measurement to use in order to collect accurate and relevant data. Here are some measurement strategies to make the process a bit easier.

Qualitative Data

One of the main types of data to collect, especially when measuring things like employee engagement and productivity, is qualitative data. This is data that isn't easily reduced to numbers and requires methods like surveys to mine for information and translate the respondent's answers into something quantifiable.[*] There are a few different ways to collect qualitative data.

---

[*] Belyh, A., 2019. Overview of Qualitative And Quantitative Data Collection Methods. [online] Cleverism. Available at: <https://www.cleverism.com/qualitative-and-quantitative-data-collection-methods/>.

Individual Interviews

If you hope to gain some insight into how specific employees are doing, individual interviews are a good option. This might be a good choice if you are curious about how a particular change has impacted specific employees in the workplace as this method is often used to collect highly personalized information. Make sure you prepare specific and measurable questions to ask ahead of time and keep the interview friendly and casual in order to make sure you receive answers that are truthful rather than answers your employee believes you want to hear. The format of this book, with the scenes between a CEO and his select employees, should help you develop the tone.

Surveys and Questionnaires

For broader feedback, surveys and questionnaires are a good option. These methods are designed to collect standardized data, making them the go-to choice for workplace feedback that provides a broad overview. These surveys and questionnaires can be conducted online or in person, and the right option for your business depends on your employees and their comfort zones. If your business is heavily online or otherwise on computers, then using electronic surveys might be the easiest choice. If that familiarity with technology is missing, however, written or in-person questionnaires might be the better options. There are many qualified survey companies to do this for your organization. In fact, having used many in the past, I recommend retaining them versus the HR department taking on this burden. The survey companies are specialists in this space and can decisively design questionnaires that will get you the answers you need. They have the experience to get the best results.

Quantitative Data

While we're a bit more interested in qualitative data collection in this chapter, quantitative data is equally important. It's also a bit more straightforward than qualitative collection as it requires less interpretation of the results and relies more on statistical analysis of the numbers. Much of this can be accomplished by taking numbers that already exist—financial records, for example—and looking at how the numbers interact with each other.[*] If you need

---

[*]   Thehartford.com. n.d. Market Research: Quantitative Vs. Qualitative Research | The Hartford. [online] Available at: <https://www.thehartford.com/business-insurance/strategy/market-research/quantitative-qualitative>.

to collect new data, you can use the same methods described above, however the questions on surveys and questionnaires should be close-ended such as those on a demographic survey. The goal isn't to collect opinions but rather straightforward information that can be compiled and analyzed.

Additional methods of quantitative data collection include:[*]

- Absolute number
- Relative number
- Percent of target
- Rate of change
- Percent of forecast
- Multivariate functions

These are all different ways to interpret data in order to find the information most relevant to your needs. The option you select will depend upon what you are hoping to examine.

Both quantitative and qualitative data are important for your business. In general, surveys collecting qualitative data, such as engagement or productivity surveys, will be most useful to analyze your workforce. Quantitative data, on the other hand, is more commonly used to locate and interpret trends or to determine how a change is impacting your bottom line.

Can You Manage What You Can't Measure?

Measuring as much as possible is an important step forward, but is it true that if you can't measure something, you can't manage it? Not necessarily. Quantifying everything you can gives you the ability to make smart decisions driven by data as well as the means by which to definitively measure your progress toward the goal. This is absolutely vital in effecting lasting change. With that said, however, you shouldn't give up on managing something simply because you cannot immediately measure it. You are the leader of the organization and that's for a good reason. You have good instincts. Trust those and go with them even if the data doesn't support it. One of the

---

[*]   Eckfeldt, B., 2018. Effective Management Requires Good Metrics. Here Are 11 Types You Need to Know. [online] Inc.com. Available at: <https://www.inc.com/bruce-eckfeldt/you-cant-manage-what-you-dont-measure-here-are-11-ways-to-measure-any-aspect-of-your-business.html>.

reasons Steve Jobs was such a great success is that he didn't rely on testing nor data on something he knew was right and would work.

It is important to not fall into the idea that numbers are the most important factor that should play a part in your decision-making. While you can certainly use them to help inform yourself, you should be making calls based on what you know of yourself, your employees, and your business, too. Everything is not quantifiable. The impact you have on a new hire, for example, and how your encouragement improves and bolsters their performance, isn't something that is immediately able to be measured. It's something that you have to do on faith and wait until later to see what patterns emerge in the productivity and passion of the employees and their careers with you.

Numbers are only one part of the equation. If you do some research and find that the data says you should do one thing but all of your experience and knowledge in the industry say that doing so would be the wrong call, take some time before you make a decision. Think about the methods you used to collect data, what that data says about the issue in question, and how your experience stacks up against all of that information. Sometimes the answer might be that you believe something is working "well enough" and don't want to disrupt things—if this is the case, it might just be a good idea to move forward regardless. But if you can see flaws in the numbers or have questions about the accuracy of the data you collected, pause on the decision-making and instead refine your measurements. Restructure and recreate the questions you're asking if using a survey to measure something, for example, to better reflect the issue at hand. Sometimes the information you collect doesn't reflect the problem or topic in question because the technique used isn't accurate.

Use your common sense as you move forward. There is a difference between using data to inform your decisions as much as possible and blindly following the numbers against all reason. Some things can be difficult to measure—some might not be accurately measurable at all. Move cautiously in these situations and weigh your choices and options before taking a step forward and implementing any changes. Consider talking to coworkers or colleagues about the dilemma and asking them for their input. This kind of informal information gathering can be incredibly helpful when it comes to organizing your thoughts and considering new perspectives.

Sometimes you have to make a call based on experience rather than data, and that's okay. It doesn't mean that you can't control the issue simply because it can't be measured—it means that it requires more attention and care than other decisions might. And keep in mind that sometimes the best way to measure these things is to look at what they impact. If you make a decision to change something in the office and its impact cannot easily be measured, take a look elsewhere. Does that change impact morale? Will it affect productivity? How have those two measurable factors changed?

The Next 24 Hours

Now that you have an idea about how to collect data and why doing so is important as you move forward, let's look at the next 24 hours and how you can begin putting everything you've learned into action. Don't worry—this information might seem a bit overwhelming, but in practice it's fairly straightforward. The first thing you want to do, as mentioned earlier in the chapter, is determine your baseline. This is your starting point and "control" group, the information against which all future data will be measured.

You should create an engagement survey to explore your baseline and determine how to move forward. This will help you gauge how your employees are interacting with their work and perhaps even with each other as well as provide insights that might allow you to more easily chart a plan of action. Once you have that information in hand, you can begin making changes and measuring how they are impacting your business by comparing new results to the baseline.

Keep the information from the previous chapters in mind as you move forward. The ultimate goal is to create an environment that encourages people to work smarter, not harder, and fosters creativity and productivity. This is best done by creating a plan personalized to your business. How can you incorporate the five components that are essential to increasing your productivity and streamlining your business operations while maintaining your workplace culture?

Once you have the baseline secured and have implemented your changes, stay the course and send the survey out again six months later. Make sure you're using the same survey you used first! It's important to keep this measurement identical so that the information you collect from each survey is directly comparable to the information and data collected from prior surveys. This tactic will pay off as time passes and the number of surveys to sort through increases exponentially.

Once you have the updated information, look at how it has changed when compared to your baseline. This should give you the information you need to determine if the changes are working—and if they aren't, you can use that information to design a better plan with the additional knowledge at your disposal. Don't be discouraged if not everything is perfect right away—it often takes a few tries to get it right.

So there you have it. Everything in this book is here to help make you and the organization more productive. Now, as a final incentive, I'm going to show you below the potential and reward of your hard work in getting your organization and yourself to be more productive. The chart below should give you incentive to start using the tools in this book. Don't leave money on the table. Start the process of increasing productivity. Work Smart Now!

The Business Case (Sum Total)

Here is the sum total of the ROI in adopting the changes in your organization from the ideas in this book. These are conservative estimates based on research and data. I did not manufacture these numbers. They are all

WORK SMART NOW Annual Total Return On Investment (ROI) Company of 1, 000 employees	
1. Absence Mgt	$3,250,000
2. Presenteeism Mgt	$10,200,000
3. Well-being	$270,000
4. Engagement	$9,595,800
5. Technology	$18,750,000
6. Optimizing your workday	$261,000,000
Totals	$303,065,800

substantiated by an abundance of data from dozens of organizations. The amount of money to be gained is substantial. I hope this is enough motivation to get you started. These significant results can benefit any organization. The precepts in this book are all laid out for you, so take advantage of them. They are the culmination of more than four decades of experience.

Final Note to the Reader

If you've made it this far, I congratulate you and thank you. You would have not read this book if you didn't want to make change in your organization. And I also know that if you have completed this book, you want to leave a positive imprint and legacy in the world. You are on your way!

You can start with one section, but your strategy and timeline should include all the productivity buckets in this book. Piecemeal will not get you where you need to go. As Aristotle said 2,732 years ago, "The whole is greater than the sum of the parts." The synergy of doing these changes together will increase its value that you cannot measure. Aristotle was one of our first and best human resources gurus.

Keep the following in mind as you proceed to take action from the tenets of this book:

- Get your house in order first. Nothing in this book will help your organization if you don't have solid business fundamentals in place: good leadership and management, finance, recruitment, etc.
- Get your personal life in order. That means your mental health, too.
- Get healthy; stay healthy. You are no good to anyone if you are not healthy.
- Set an example. Don't respond to emails after business hours unless it is a critical issue.
- Create the position of Director of Productivity to drive the initiative.

I leave you with a quote from a brilliant 19th-century rabbi, Israel Salanter: "When I was a young man, I wanted to change the world. I found it difficult to change the world, so I tried to change my nation. When I found I couldn't change the nation, I began to focus on my town. I couldn't change the town, so, as an older man, I tried to change my family. Now, as an old man, I realize that the only thing I can change is myself. And suddenly I realize that if, long ago, I had changed myself, I could have made an impact on my family. My family could have made an impact on our town. The town's impact could have changed the nation, and I could indeed have changed the world."

APPENDIX
Further Reading

A: Further Reading on Chapter Two (Introducing Productivity)

Adaa.org. n.d. Highlights: Workplace Stress & Anxiety Disorders Survey | Anxiety and Depression Association of America, ADAA. [online] Available at: <https://adaa.org/workplace-stress-anxiety-disorders-survey>

This article recounts ADAA statistics about the mental health of American employees and notes that actual diagnosis rates are markedly lower than they perhaps should be. From the source text:

> It comes as no surprise that most working Americans experience stress or anxiety in their daily lives. And the Anxiety Disorders Association of America (ADAA) 2006 Stress & Anxiety Disorders Survey backs that up. A certain amount of stress and anxiety is normal at work as well as at home. However, persistent, excessive, and irrational anxiety that interferes with everyday functioning is often an indication of an anxiety disorder. Read on for now how stress affects American employees.
>
> [. . .]
>
> Self-reporting of anxiety symptoms and prescription medication use are high among America's employees, but diagnoses of anxiety disorders are dramatically lower. 72 percent of people who have daily stress and anxiety say it interferes with their lives at least moderately. 40 percent experience persistent stress or excessive anxiety in their daily lives. 30 percent with daily stress have taken prescription medication to manage stress, nervousness, emotional problems or lack of sleep.

Blog.mavenlink.com. 2020. Mavenlink Future of Work Survey Shows 47 percent of Employees Feel Lazy Coworkers Are Number-One Pet Peeve. [online] Available at: <https://blog.mavenlink.com/press/mavenlink-future-work-survey-lazy-coworkers-number-one-pet-peeve>

This article looks at survey results from Mavelink's Future of Work. It calls into question the wisdom of maintaining some traditional work elements, taking a critical look at their impact on employee productivity. From the source text:

Mavenlink, the leading provider of cloud-based software for the modern services organization, today announced new results from its inaugural "Future of Work" survey about generational differences in the modern workplace. The first release focused on the importance of work/life balance. This second data release examines how organizations can develop team-building opportunities, another of the top three most important workplace elements.

[. . .]

Meetings are universally loathed, especially by older cohorts. "Too many/unnecessary meetings" (41 percent all) was the third-most selected productivity killer. The 45 to 54-year-old (46 percent) and 55 to 64-year-old (50 percent) age groups differ here. Both selected "too many/unnecessary meetings" as their first-choice productivity killer and at higher rates than the entire sample size.

Boyarsky, K., 2019. Productivity: The Ultimate Guide to Getting Things Done. [online] Owllabs.com. Available at: <https://www.owllabs.com /blog/productivity>

This article explores effective time management techniques to help boost productivity in the workplace. From the source text:

It can feel more difficult than ever to be productive. There are just too many distractions, particularly when it comes to technology— we have Instagram feeds to peruse, podcasts to listen to, and Netflix shows to binge, all typically right at our fingertips. Technology has severely decreased our ability to focus. In fact, the average person's attention span has dropped from 12 seconds, in 2000, to a mere eight seconds today. Eight seconds of focus before we become distracted— how is anyone supposed to get anything done?

Ultimately, time chunking enables you to eliminate distractions by choosing time periods and ensuring you only focus on one task during that time period. Plus, it removes the time you waste jumping back and forth between tasks. The less time you spend returning to your task after a momentary distraction, the better. According to a study by Florida State University, productivity and performance are at their peak during uninterrupted 90-minute intervals—so, when in doubt, try chunking your time into 90-minute segments, and then move onto the next task after that.

Laurano, M., 2015. The True Cost of a Bad Hire. [online] Brandon Hall Group. Available at: <https://b2b-assets.glassdoor.com/the-true-cost-of -a-bad-hire.pdf>
This report explores the increasing difficulty of effective hiring in a global workforce as well as how poor hires impact office productivity. From the source text:

> 95 percent of organizations of all sizes admit to making bad hires every year, according to Brandon Hall Group's 2015 Talent Acquisition Study. These decisions can cost organizations hundreds of thousands of dollars. How can companies become smarter about their hiring decisions? How can companies mitigate the cost of a bad hire? This report will help organizations understand what is behind bad hiring decisions and key recommendations to mitigate these costs.
>
> Organizations that lack a standard interview process are five times as likely to make a bad hire. Organizations that invest in a strong candidate experience improve their quality of hires by 70 percent. Organizations that invest in employer branding are three times more likely to make a quality hire.

Mankins, M., 2017. Great Companies Obsess over Productivity, Not Efficiency. [online] *Harvard Business Review*. Available at: <https://hbr .org/2017/03/great-companies-obsess-over-productivity-not-efficiency>
This article details the difference between productivity and efficiency, emphasizing the former over the latter with examples from various studies and surveys. From the source text:

> Business leaders often think of "efficiency" and "productivity" as synonyms, two sides of the same coin. When it comes to strategy, however, efficiency and productivity are very different. At a time when so many companies are starved for growth, senior leaders must bring a productivity mindset to their business and remove organizational obstacles to workforce productivity. This view differs substantially

from the relentless focus on efficiency that has characterized management thinking for most of the last three decades, but it is absolutely
essential if companies are going to spur innovation and reignite profitable growth.

[. . .]

In the coming decade, it will be critical for business leaders to
adopt a productivity mindset. Instead of focusing on continuously
managing the denominator, by cutting headcount, executives should
identify ways to boost the numerator, and increase output. By systematically removing obstacles to productivity, deploying talent strategically, and inspiring a larger percentage of their workforce, leaders can
dramatically improve productivity and reignite top-line growth.

**Mindsharepartners.lpages.co. 2019. Mind Share Partners | Mental
Health At Work 2019 Report. [online] Available at: <https://mind
sharepartners.lpages.co/mentalhealthatworkreport2019/>**

This report examines mental health in the workplace and the ways in
which it impacts employees and employers alike as well as how it goes unde-
tected and untreated. From the source text:

While countries like the United Kingdom, Canada, and Australia
have made substantial progress in awareness of and support for mental health in the workplace, the US is only just beginning. Research
on the prevalence of mental health challenges and stigma, specifically in the workplace setting, is limited. Prevalence is often measured
either through diagnosable conditions or general stress levels, which
does not fully capture the breadth of the mental health experience.
Our report aims to broaden the current understanding of the mental health experience and its impact on workplaces and employees
beyond diagnostic prevalence.

[. . .]

60 percent of respondents reported symptoms of a mental health
condition in the past year. 20 percent of respondents had willingly left
a previous role for mental health reasons. People are 2x more likely to
be willing to give support for a colleague's mental health than ever
talk about their own challenges.

B: Further Reading on Chapter Three (Absenteeism and Presenteeism)

Bloom, N., J. Liang, J. Roberts, and J. Zhichun, 2014. Does Working from Home Work? Evidence from a Chinese Experiment. [online] Stanford University. Available at: <https://nbloom.people.stanford .edu/sites/g/files/sbiybj4746/f/wfh.pdf>

This source finds that telecommuters are 14 percent more productive than their office-bound colleagues according to a study released by Stanford University. Research found that working from home increases job performance and productivity while also decreasing the number of sick days taken. From the source text:

> We report the results of a WFH experiment at Ctrip, a 16,000-employee, NASDAQ-listed Chinese travel agency. Call center employees who volunteered to WFH were randomly assigned either to work from home or in the office for nine months. Home working led to a 13 percent performance increase, of which 9 percent was from working more minutes per shift (fewer breaks and sick days) and 4 percent from more calls per minute (attributed to a quieter and more convenient working environment).

Boyd, D., 2020. Workplace Stress—The American Institute of Stress. [online] The American Institute of Stress. Available at: <https://www .stress.org/workplace-stress>

This survey explores why job stress is an increasingly significant source of stress for the workforce in general and how such high levels of stress impact mental health and worker productivity. From the source text:

> Numerous studies show that job stress is far and away the major source of stress for American adults and that it has escalated progressively over the past few decades. Increased levels of job stress as assessed by the perception of having little control but lots of demands have been demonstrated to be associated with increased rates of heart attack, hypertension, and other disorders. . . . Job stress is costly. Job Stress carries a price tag for U.S. industry estimated at over $300 billion

annually as a result of: Accidents, absenteeism, employee turn-over, diminished productivity, direct medical, legal, and insurance costs, and workers' compensation awards as well as tort and FELA judgments.

Carmichael, S., 2015. The Research Is Clear: Long Hours Backfire for People and for Companies. [online] *Harvard Business Review*. Available at: <https://hbr.org/2015/08/the-research-is-clear-long-hours-backfire -for-people-and-for-companies>
This text looks at how overwork and burnout can significantly impact the whole of a business, including profits and employee productivity and health, as well as why such issues are still a problem in the workplace despite abundant evidence of their harm. From the source text:

> Considerable evidence shows that overwork is not just neutral—it hurts us and the companies we work for. Numerous studies of the Finnish Institute of Occupational Health (as well as other studies) have found that overwork and the resulting stress can lead to all sorts of health problems, including impaired sleep, depression, heavy drinking, diabetes, impaired memory, and heart disease. Of course, those are bad on their own. But they're also terrible for a company's bottom line, showing up as absenteeism, turnover, and rising health insurance costs.

CoSo Cloud | Secure Virtual Training & Collaboration. 2015. Press Release | CoSo Cloud Survey Shows Working Remotely Benefits Employers and Employees. [online] Available at: <https://www.cosocloud .com/press-releases/connectsolutions-survey-shows-working-remotely -benefits-employers-and-employees>
This source looks at how remote work positively impacts worker productivity, including improving the number of sick employees able to work from home rather than taking PTO. From the source text:

> Whether remote workers are able to work with greater efficiency off-site or are more motivated to demonstrate off-site effectiveness, of the 39 percent who work remotely at least a few times per month,

77 percent report greater productivity while working off site with 30 percent accomplishing more in less time and 24 percent accomplishing more in the same amount of time. 23 percent are even willing to work longer hours than they normally would on site to accomplish more while 52 percent are less likely to take time off when working remotely—even when sick.

Cushard, B., 2020. The Impact of Absenteeism. [online] ADP. Available at: <https://www.adp.com/spark/articles/2017/01/the-impact-of-absenteeism .aspx#>

This source examines the impact of presenteeism and absenteeism on the workplace as a whole, from lost profit to reduced everyday productivity on an individual level. From the source text:

> According to the Bureau of Labor Statistics (BLS), the absence rate from work for full-time employees is 2.9 percent. The impact of absenteeism is certainly a big enough problem that organizations should understand how it affects individual, team and organizational performance.

Health & Safety Ontario. 2011. [online] Available at: <https://www .wsps.ca/WSPS/media/Site/Resources/Downloads/BusinessCaseHW _Final.pdf?ext=.pdf>

This study examines healthy workplace elements and how adopting them positively impacts employees in many different areas of their life. This, in turn, illustrates how much more productive and happy employees are able to accomplish when compared with their burnt-out counterparts. From the source text:

> It is intuitively obvious that unhealthy, stressed employees will cost a company something in terms of absenteeism and decreased productivity. But a business case requires more than a "gut feeling" about issues. There is much evidence documenting the costs to business of having employees who exhibit unhealthy lifestyles (see Unhealthy Lifestyles, below). In addition, there is a growing abundance of data documenting that the organizational culture, especially certain psychosocial

risk factors, can have a profoundly negative impact on employees' health, safety, and well-being.

[. . .]

The issue of mental health warrants its own article. Here are just a few numbers: Costs of lost productivity due to mental illness in Canadian businesses equal $11.1 billion per year. Mental health problems cost Canadian businesses $33 billion per year, if non-clinical diagnoses are included (e.g. burnout, sub clinical depression, etc.). The leading cause of short-term and long-term disability in 2005 was mental health issues, including stress.

Health Advocate, 2009. Stress in the Workplace: Meeting the Challenge. [online] Available at: <http://healthadvocate.com/downloads/webinars /stress-workplace.pdf>

This source examines how stress impacts individuals as well as organizations and offers detailed information about the financial as well as emotional costs of the issue. From the source text:

This white paper offers comprehensive research about the causes and impact of workplace stress, its role in lost productivity and higher healthcare costs and includes the effects of job stress on women workers. The research also reviews successful organizational and individual strategies to help manage stress and reduce costs. Following these strategies can help reduce absenteeism and turnover, help employees better balance work/life responsibilities, and also reduce healthcare costs.

Additionally, the text notes that absenteeism and presenteeism cost employers almost $150 billion every year. From the source text:

Presenteeism manifests in a host of ways, including making mistakes, more time spent on tasks, poor quality work, impaired social functioning, burnout, anger, resentment, low morale and other detrimental factors. Overall, the price tag related to presenteeism adds up to nearly $150 billion a year in lost productivity, according to the international Foundation of employee Benefit Plans. the cost may be even higher if the stress underlying presenteeism is not addressed, as absenteeism, job resignations, chronic illness, and disability may be the result.

Kessler, R., M. Petukhova, and K. McInnes, (2007). World Health Organization Health and Work Performance Questionnaire (HPQ). HPQ Short Form (Absenteeism and Presenteeism Questions and Scoring Rules) Harvard Medical School. Available at: <hcp.med.harvard.edu/ hpq/ftpdir/absenteeism%20presenteeism%20scoring%20050107.pdf.>

This source looks at the absenteeism and presenteeism questions created by the World Health Organization in detail and discusses scoring rules to accurately interpret information gathered using them. From the source text:

A number of researchers have asked whether they can abstract the absenteeism and presenteeism questions from the full HPQ and use these questions alone or in conjunction with another interview. This memo lists the questions that are needed to do this and describes the scoring rules for the absenteeism and presenteeism measures based on this core set of HPQ questions.

Lorenz, M., 2015. How Much Does Temperature Affect Your Productivity? | Careerbuilder. [online] Careerbuilder.com. Available at: <https://www.careerbuilder.com/advice/how-much-does-temperature -affect-your-productivity>

This source takes a bit of a different approach and examines how factors like office temperature impact productivity and engagement. From the source text:

According to a new CareerBuilder survey, the office temperature is the source of some (ahem) heated debate among workers across the country. One in five workers (20 percent) have argued with a co-worker about the office temperature being either too hot or too cold, and 18 percent have secretly changed the temperature during the winter (sneaky!).

[. . .]

Fighting over the number on the thermostat may seem like a petty office squabble, but the majority of workers feel that office temperature can affect their ability to work effectively. According to the survey: 53 percent of employees say they are less productive when working in an office that is too cold. 71 percent say they are less productive when working in an office that is too warm.

Loubier, A., 2017. Benefits of Telecommuting for the Future of Work. [online] *Forbes*. Available at: <https://www.forbes.com/sites /andrealoubier/2017/07/20/benefits-of-telecommuting-for-the-future -of-work/#64f1bb5b16c6>

This source details the results of a U.K. survey regarding stress while working and how remote work helps to avoid or reduce its severity. From the source text:

In a report published by the Royal Society for Public Health in the UK, it found that 55 percent of people felt more stressed as a result of their commute. Snacking habits also increased and with less free time available, the report also found that workers were leading less active and healthy lifestyles.

In a 2014 study by PGi, a leading provider of software services, it found that 80 percent of remote workers reported higher morale, 82 percent said it helped lower their stress levels, and 69 percent reported lower absenteeism.

McLaren, S., 2019. How These 4 Companies Are Embracing Flexible Work—And Why You Should Too. [online] Business.linkedin.com. Available at: <https://business.linkedin.com/talent-solutions/blog/work -flexibility/2019/how-4-companies-are-embracing-flexible-work>

This source details why some of the most prominent global companies are making the decision to offer employees flexible work schedules. From the source text:

A third (31 percent) of LinkedIn users say flexible work arrangements are a very important consideration when choosing a job. That's a third of candidates who might turn down an offer if your company doesn't offer flexibility. That's according to LinkedIn's Global Talent Trends 2019 report, which surveyed 5,000 talent acquisition and HR professionals around the world. And although 36 percent of women and 29 percent of men say flexibility really matters when they make job decisions, fears about communication, productivity, and lack of oversight hold many companies back from fully embracing these desirable policies.

Today, Dell offers a variety of flexible work options, allowing employees to work remotely some or all of the time, and at variable hours. The program has been a huge success, with nearly 60 percent of employees working flexibly and reporting a Net Promoter Score that's typically 20 percent higher than those who don't. And with fewer people in the office every day, Dell doesn't need as much office space—netting the company $12 million in annual savings since 2014.

Press Room | Career Builder. 2017. Do American Workers Need a Vacation? New Careerbuilder Data Shows Majority Are Burned Out at Work, While Some Are Highly Stressed or Both. [online] Available at: <http://press.careerbuilder.com/2017-05-23-Do-American-Workers -Need-a-Vacation-New-CareerBuilder-Data-Shows-Majority-Are -Burned-Out-at-Work-While-Some-Are-Highly-Stressed-or-Both>
This source details why employees are leaving vacation time untouched despite being stressed and experiencing burnout. From the source text:

If you can't remember the last time you took a vacation, you're not alone. While American workers are stressed, they're not taking time away from work. According to a new CareerBuilder survey, 3 in 5 workers (61 percent) say they are burned out in their current job, and 31 percent report high or extremely high levels of stress at work, yet a third of all workers (33 percent) have not taken or do not plan to take a vacation this year.

[. . .]

When workers do take advantage of vacation time, they are often not fully disconnecting from their jobs—3 in 10 (31 percent) check work email while away and nearly a fifth (18 percent) check in with work. More than a third (36 percent) say that they've returned from vacation to find so much work, they wish they'd never left at all, and 18 percent say vacations cause them to be more stressed out about work. This could be the reason nearly 1 in 5 (17 percent) left vacation days on the table at the end of last year.

Shepherd, M., 2020. 28 Surprising Working from Home Statistics. [online] Fundera. Available at: <https://www.fundera.com/resources /working-from-home-statistics>
This source looks at remote work before and after COVID-19 and explains how the pandemic has permanently impacted how employers and employees alike view remote work. From the source text:

Even before the coronavirus outbreak forced businesses across the world to adopt a remote work policy, there were over 5 million US employees working from home at least half the time. Now, telecommuting is more popular than ever—whether people were prepared for it or not.
[. . .]
Having employee productivity issues in the workplace? Work from home statistics suggest that telecommuters are more productive workers. Two-thirds of managers report that employees who work from home increase their overall productivity. Even more, 86 percent of employees say they're most productive when they work alone—devoid of distractions like inefficient meetings, office gossip, or loud office spaces.

Smith, S., 2016. Presenteeism Costs Business 10 Times More than Absenteeism. [online] EHS Today. Available at: <https://www.ehstoday .com/safety-leadership/article/21918281/presenteeism-costs -business-10-times-more-than-absenteeism>
This source explores the business costs of presenteeism and why it might be a costlier issue than absenteeism alone. From the source text:

On average, employees cost businesses the equivalent of three months per year in lost productivity, according to a new GCC Insights report by Global Corporate Challenge (GCC). GCC's study on presentee-ism—the phenomenon where employees show up for work but don't perform at full capacity—included nearly 2,000 employees and validated against the World Health Organization (WHO) Workplace Health and Productivity Questionnaire (HPQ).

Stahl, A., 2016. Here's What Burnout Costs You. [online] *Forbes*. Available at: <https://www.forbes.com/sites/ashleystahl/2016/03/04 /heres-what-burnout-costs-you/#66c286d44e05>
This article examines the sheer financial impact of employee burnout through a variety of factors. From the source text:

> If you think you may be burnt out, know that you're not alone. Stressed, burnt-out employees are prevalent in the professional world today, and it costs employers a lot, whether it's due to increased health-care costs, loss of productivity, or employees calling off. As many as one million people per day miss work because of stress. Studies suggest that all of this translates into a loss of anywhere from $150 billion to $300 billion annually for US employers. The effects of burnout take a toll not only on individuals, but also on businesses and the economy.

Wilkie, D., 2017. Workplace Burnout at 'Epidemic Proportions.' [online] SHRM. Available at: <https://www.shrm.org/resourcesandtools/hr-topics /employee-relations/pages/employee-burnout.aspx>
This article explains why employee burnout is negatively impacting employee retention and job satisfaction. From the source text:

> Too much work. Too little pay. Too many technological advance-ments. Too much emphasis on recruiting new employees rather than keeping existing ones happy. All these are reasons employee burnout is perhaps worse than it has ever been, according to a new survey from Kronos Inc. and Future Workplace. . . . The survey of 614 US HR professionals, conducted by Morar Consulting from Nov. 14–19, 2016, found that 95 percent of HR leaders said employee burnout is sabotaging workforce retention. The survey targeted HR managers and directors, vice presidents of HR, and chief HR officers—all of

them working at organizations with at least 100 employees. Unfair compensation (41 percent), unreasonable workload (32 percent), and too much overtime or after-hours work (32 percent) were the top three contributors to burnout, respondents said.

Willis Towers Watson. 2020. The Mounting Crisis of Mental Health. [online] Available at: <https://www.willistowerswatson.com/en-US/Insights /2019/11/the-mounting-crisis-of-mental-health>
This survey report explores how many employees are suffering from mental health issues of some sort and how this impacts their productivity as well as what can be done to help alleviate some of their struggles to better enable them to work at their full potential. From the source text:

The scale of this crisis is such that it has received in-depth attention from the World Health Organization (WHO), which led to a 2013–2020 action plan for participating states. . . . Both a wider statistical basis to the concerns about mental health and a series of more specific figures of direct interest to employers are revealed in the survey: Mental health disorders are common in the workforce globally; around 3 in 10 employees suffer from severe stress, anxiety or depression. Over 300 million people of all ages suffer from depression globally.

C: Further Reading on Chapter Four (Well-Being)

American Psychological Association, 2016. Workplace Well-Being Linked to Senior Leadership Support, New Survey Finds. Available at: <https://www.apa.org/news/press/releases/2016/06/workplace-well-being>

This source examines a recent study regarding workplace well-being and how it impacts job satisfaction, employee retention, and productivity, among others. From the source text:

> Nearly three-fourths (73 percent) of employees with senior managers who show support through involvement and commitment to well-being initiatives said their organization helps employees develop a healthy lifestyle, compared with just 11 percent who work in an organization without that leadership support, according to APA's 2016 Work and Well-Being Survey (PDF, 726KB). It was conducted online by Harris Poll among more than 1,500 US adults in March.
>
> The survey found widespread links between support from senior leaders and a variety of employee and organizational outcomes, with more than 9 in 10 workers saying they feel motivated to do their best (91 percent vs. 38 percent of those without leadership support), are satisfied with their job (91 percent vs. 30 percent) and have a positive relationship with supervisors (91 percent vs. 54 percent) and coworkers (93 percent vs. 72 percent). These employees are also more likely to recommend their company as a good place to work (89 percent vs. 17 percent) and fewer said they intend to leave their job in the next year (25 percent vs. 51 percent).

Business.com Editorial Staff, 2020. Why You Need to Worry About Employee Burnout. [online] Available at: <https://www.business.com/articles/why-you-need-to-worry-about-burnout/>

This source collates information from numerous studies and surveys about employee burnout and productivity, using it to present a synthesized view of the problems. From the source text:

> Chronic fatigue, disengagement, low motivation, and poor performance—these are just some telltale signs of employee burnout that

companies need to pay close attention to. Employee burnout is not a personal issue or an indicator of incompetence. Rather, it is a challenge that needs to be tackled from an organizational level. Workplace stress, in fact, is primarily caused by ineffective leadership and flawed organizational practices.

[. . .]

A mounting body of research demonstrates a positive correlation between an employee's health and well-being and their productivity at work. A study conducted by the U.K. government shows that positive employee well-being results in improved performance, productivity and work quality. Another study conducted by IZA World of Labor claims that an increase in employee well-being leads to parallel increases in productivity. These studies show that an employee's health and well-being play a critical role in the quality of the outputs they produce. Simply put, an employee who is healthy and well-rested is more likely to deliver high-quality output compared to an employee struggling with a demanding workload.

CPA Practice Advisor. 2020. 38 Percent Of U.S. Workers Live Paycheck to Paycheck. [online] Available at: <https://www.cpapracticeadvisor.com /payroll/news/21125346/38-of-us-workers-live-paycheck-to-paycheck>
This article compiles statistics from the Global Benefits Attitudes Survey related to financial wellness and current situation American employees face. From the source text:

The Global Benefits Attitudes Survey found 43 percent of US workers are satisfied with their financial situation, an increase from 35 percent in 2017. Employee satisfaction with their finances has now recovered to levels seen between 2011 and 2015. Additionally, 4 in 10 (42 percent) say their financial situation has improved over the past two years, and nearly 6 in 10 (58 percent) believe their finances are heading in the right direction. However, the survey revealed some worrisome findings:

Thirty-eight percent of employees live paycheck to paycheck. 39 percent of employees could not come up with $3,000 if an unexpected need arose within the next month. 18 percent of employees making more than $100,000 annually live paycheck to paycheck.

70 percent of employees are saving less for retirement than they think they should. 32 percent of employees have financial problems that negatively affect their lives. 64 percent of employees believe their generation is likely to be much worse off in retirement than that of their parents.

IFEBP, 2017. Workplace Wellness Goes Beyond ROI. Available at: <https://www.ifebp.org/aboutus/pressroom/releases/Pages/Workplace-Wellness-Goes-Beyond-ROI-.aspx>

This study examines not only how wellness impacts workplaces but also how employers are going above and beyond to establish smart wellness tactics for their employees. From the source text:

> Employers are trading return on investment (ROI) numbers for the prevalence of worker health and well-being when it comes to workplace wellness programs. Continued increases in productivity and decreases in absenteeism strengthen the case for workplace wellness programs, according to findings from the International Foundation of Employee Benefit Plans Workplace Wellness 2017 Survey Report. The survey found 75 percent of employers offer wellness initiatives primarily to improve overall worker health and well-being. Only one in four employers said the main reason for offering wellness initiatives is to control/reduce health-related costs.
>
> [. . .]
>
> Among employers offering and measuring their wellness efforts, more than half have found a decrease in absenteeism, 63 percent are experiencing financial sustainability and growth in the organization, 66 percent reported increased productivity and 67 percent said employees are more satisfied. According to the survey, 77 percent of employers offer free or discounted flu shots, so traditional wellness offerings continue to gain steam.

James, G., 2016. 9 Reasons That Open-Space Offices Are Insanely Stupid. [online] Inc.com. Available at: <https://www.inc.com/geoffrey-james/why-your-company-will-benefit-from-getting-rid-of-open-office-spaces-first-90.html>

This article looks at mounting evidence against open-space offices, exploring why they are ultimately far more detrimental than helpful and how they negatively impact the employees using them. From the source text:

> Open-plan offices (large open spaces, shared work areas, and few private offices) are all the rage. In fact, approximately 70 percent of all offices now have an open floor plan. . . . Contrary to popular belief, open offices don't increase collaboration or make people more productive. An Exeter University study showed they create a 32 percent drop in "workers' well-being" and 15 percent reduction in productivity. . . . A study of 10,000 workers funded by office furniture giant Steelcase revealed that "95 percent said working privately was important to them, but only 41 percent said they could do so, and 31 percent had to leave the office to get work completed."

Kupka, A., 2012. Why You Need to Love Your Job. [online] Forbes. Available at: <https://www.forbes.com/sites/annakupka/2012/01/26/why-you-need-to-love-your-job/#15f0d97077cd>

> Loving one's job is not only a "rare-to-find-nice-to-have", no, it is essential for our entire society and for our overall well-being. The workplace is the place where we spend most our waking time and people hating their jobs is throughout the world one of the main reasons for economic downturns. If we would all use our unique talents to serve humanity (and we all have these talents!), there would be no unemployment and no stress-related illnesses. I have heard of a woman who makes her living plucking eyebrows. Nothing else—just plucking eyebrows. Based in New York, she is such an amazing eyebrow plucker that celebrities from around the world queue to avail of her services. If you can make a very good living by plucking eyebrows, you can make a living of anything! Or as Albert Schweitzer said: "Success is not the key to happiness. Happiness is the key to success. If you love what you are doing, you will be successful."

O'Keefe, P., 2014. Liking Work Really Matters. [online] Nytimes.com. Available at: <https://www.nytimes.com/2014/09/07/opinion/sunday/go-with-the-flow.html?_r=0>

Research by the psychologists Chris S. Hulleman of the University of Virginia and Judith Harackiewicz of the University of Wisconsin suggests that for most of us, whether we find something interesting is largely a matter of whether we find it personally valuable. For many students, science is boring because they don't think it's relevant to their lives.

With this in mind, the researchers asked high school science students to periodically do some writing over the course of a semester. They randomly selected half of them to summarize what they had learned in their class. The other half wrote about the usefulness of science in their own lives, thereby making it personally relevant and valuable. At the end of the semester, the researchers found that, compared with those who simply summarized the material, the ones who reflected on its personal relevance reported more interest in science—as well as significantly higher grades, on average by almost a full grade point. This was particularly true for those with the lowest expectations for performing well in their class.

Paycor.com. 2018. Does Employee Morale Boost Revenue? [online] Available at: <https://www.paycor.com/resource-center/does-employee-morale-boost-revenue>

This source examines various causes of low morale in the workplace, its impact upon the overall health and efficiency of a company, and solutions designed to permanently boost morale. From the source text:

If your company is having a low-morale crisis, you have several options to right the ship. One success formula is to make sure you've got the right employees in the right jobs, and that you've gone above and beyond to keep them there. Although a great salary, benefits, and bonuses and perks are one way to help ensure your people stay happy, the quality of work/life issues is a vital element that has a definite and measurable impact on their morale and results in successful contributions.

[. . .]

Let 'em Sleep. Say what, now? According to a study conducted by scientists at the University of California, San Diego, naps are more effective than caffeine for increasing alertness and promoting learning on some memory tasks. Creating a space for workplace naps can be as simple as designating an unused office as a nap room and fitting it with a reclining chair. However, those with a bigger budget can invest in a fleet of nap pods.

Poswolsky, A., 2016. How to Start Loving Your Job Again. [online] *Time.* **Available at: <https://time.com/4513661/job-happiness-success-advice/> [Accessed 2 September 2020].**

In *The Quarter-Life Breakthrough*, I tell the stories of numerous mean-ing-hungry millennials who actually found they were happier when they quit being a solopreneur (someone working for themselves), and became an intrapreneur (someone working in a large company with a team). A recent Gallup report revealed that 21 percent of millenni-als have switched jobs within the past year, three times the number of nonmillennials, and only 29 percent of millennials are engaged with their jobs, making them the least engaged generation in the workplace.

If millions of Americans are disengaged at their jobs, then clearly we need to make it easier for people to experience meaning, purpose, and joy in the workplace.

PWC, 2017. Special Report: Financial Stress and the Bottom Line. [online] PWC.com. Available at: <https://www.pwc.com/us/en/private-company -services/publications/assets/pwc-financial-stress-and-bottom-line.pdf>

This report, based on PWC's 2017 Employee Financial Wellness Survey, takes a closer look at how money troubles impact employee performance. From the source text:

Financial stress can have a major impact on employees, from greater health concerns to trouble with relationships and distractions at work. This same stress can also influence a company's well-being, including potentially higher costs due to elevated healthcare plan use, lost productivity from distractions/absenteeism, and lower savings for retirement or medical expenses. This special report, based on the results of our 2017 Employee Financial Wellness Survey, delves into data around stress and its impact on the financial well-being of both the employee and employer.

[. . .]

The effect of financial stress on worker productivity is striking. Employees who are stressed about their finances are nearly five times more likely to be distracted by their finances at work, twice as likely to spend 3 hours or more at work dealing with financial matters, and three times more likely to spend five hours or more. Stressed employees are also twice as likely to miss work on account of their personal financial issues and are more inclined to cite health issues caused by financial stress. They are also more likely to experience difficulties with relationships at home.

Sun Life Financial—Group Benefits, 2012. A Strategic Dose of Wellness. Available at: <https://www.sunlife.ca/static/canada/Sponsor/About%20 Group%20Benefits/Group%20benefits%20products%20and%20services /The%20Conversation/Bright%20Papers/files/1748-03-12-e.pdf>

This survey presents the 2011 Buffett National Wellness Survey results and discusses how wellness impacts businesses and the best way to go about ensuring employee wellness. From the source text:

Launched in 1997, the Buffett National Wellness Survey is a pioneering study delivering key insights and leading trends into workplace wellness in Canada. The 2011 online survey was conducted in the spring and summer of 2011 and presents findings from a national sample of 677 Canadian employers across the public, private and non-profit sectors.

The 2011 Buffett National Wellness Survey, a national survey of Canadian employers, confirms that workplace wellness has hit the mainstream. Ninety-seven percent of survey respondents agreed that employee health is directly related to corporate success, while 72 percent reported offering at least one wellness initiative to their employees.... Health conditions—such as diabetes, heart disease, cancer and depression—continue to increase significantly, impacting organizations' productivity and causing their medical costs to escalate. The good news is that most chronic conditions are preventable. According to the World Health Organization (WHO), approximately 80 percent of heart disease and diabetes, and 40 percent of most cancers are largely preventable through proper diet, physical activity and smoking cessation.

[. . .]

Organizations with highly effective health and productivity programs report 11 percent higher revenue per employee and 28 percent greater shareholder returns.

USC MAPP Online. n.d. Liking Your Job Helps You Succeed | USC Online. [online] Available at: <https://appliedpsychologydegree.usc.edu /blog/how-liking-your-job-will-help-you-succeed/>

Steve Jobs stood in front of the 2005 Stanford graduating class and said, "the only way to do great work is to love what you do," but how does enjoying your work really lead to success in the workplace? Being happy at work and loving what you do is an overall productivity booster and enhances performance. People who enjoy their jobs are more likely to be optimistic, motivated, learn faster, make fewer mistakes, and better business decisions. . . . According to Mihaly Csikszentmihalyi, a distinguished Hungarian psychologist, being able to enjoy your work is the main factor in getting into a state of flow.

Csikszentmihalyi discovered that once you take on a task with a positive mindset and think of the benefits you can reap from completing this project, your work is more likely to happen in a steady, concentrated flow. Being in this state of mind means you will be highly focused and fully absorbed in the task at hand, just as you would be while doing something you really enjoy. Being able to fully devote yourself to a task and give it your all will make you more productive and knowledgeable, leading you toward success at work.

Virgin Pulse, 2017. 2017 State of the Industry: Employee Wellbeing, Engagement and Culture in 2017. Available at: <https://community.virginpulse.com/state-of-the-industry-2017-es>

This survey examines how wellness impacts employee engagement and how important ensuring employee health is becoming to companies across the globe. From the source text:

> Eighty-seven percent of those surveyed responded that they currently or plan to invest in employee wellbeing as part of their employee engagement strategy. Ninety-seven percent of respondents agree with the statement that wellbeing positively influences engagement. Eighty-eight percent of respondents prioritize increasing employee engagement, but there is a lack of consensus around the strategies, tactics, challenges and results achieved to date, indicating an opportunity for organizations to realize wellbeing's foundational role in driving culture, employee engagement and business performance. Eighty percent of respondents currently or will have initiatives in place in the next year to improve culture, which is critical for increasing engagement. The majority of organizations have cultural outcomes specifically in mind when designing employee engagement programs.

D: Further Reading on Chapter Five (Engagement)

ADP. n.d. Employee Engagement vs. Employee Satisfaction White Paper. [online] ADP. Available at: <https://www.adp.com/~/media/RI/whitepapers /Employee%20Engagement%20vs%20Employee%20Satisfaction%20 White%20Paper.ashx>

This white paper from ADP provides a comprehensive look at job satisfaction and employee engagement. It looks at not only the differences between the two, but also the similarities and provides a plethora of data to back up its insight. From the source text:

> So is employee engagement just a new buzz word for job satisfaction? The answer is no. Satisfaction and engagement are two important, yet distinct measurements that provide valuable and actionable insights into the workforce. The problem is that too many organizations still view them as one and the same thing. As a result, they may be missing critical opportunities to foster the kind of workforce engagement that drives innovation, boosts performance, and increases competitive success.
>
> Some organizations think they don't have to worry about engagement because turnover is low and employees seem satisfied. While employee satisfaction is important to maintaining a positive work environment, is it enough to help you retain top performers and drive bottom-line impact? Probably not. By focusing more on employee engagement, organizations are more likely to maintain a strong, motivated workforce that is willing to expend extra effort, drive business goals, and deliver a return on HR's talent management investment.
>
> This paper explores the differences between engagement and satisfaction, the importance of measuring engagement over time, as well as actionable strategies for maximizing workforce engagement and, subsequently, driving higher performance across the organization.

Autry, A., 2019. Millennial Employee Engagement & Loyalty Statistics: The Ultimate Collection. [online] Blog.accessperks.com. Available at: <https: //blog.accessperks.com/millennial-employee-engagement-loyalty -statistics-the-ultimate-collection>

This source looks at a wealth of statistics regarding millennials in the workplace, including loyalty and engagement data with links directly to the source placed beside each stat. From the source text:

Building a workplace that Millennials thrive in doesn't mean getting rid of everything that worked for previous generations. As you can see from this extensive collection, they're very traditional in some senses—they want good compensation, fair benefits, friends in the office, the chance to grow and develop, and a few corporate perks thrown in to sweeten the deal.

But their unique circumstances and background have led them to approach companies with a different perspective. For example, being raised in a layoff culture has led them to view loyalty in terms of months, not years. Also, their mobile technology-centric lifestyles have made them view the traditional, 9–5, cubicle-dwelling work arrangement as outdated. To help you decipher and engage this generation for your company's success, we've compiled every relevant piece of data about Millennials in the workplace we can find.

Clifton, J., 2017. The World's Broken Workplace. [online] Gallup.com. Available at: <https://news.gallup.com/opinion/chairman/212045/world -broken-workplace.aspx?g_source=EMPLOYEE_ENGAGEMENT>
This article explores data related to employee engagement, job satisfaction, and employee loyalty as compiled and curated by Gallup. From the source text:

Employees everywhere don't necessarily hate the company or organization they work for as much as they do their boss. Employees—especially the stars—join a company and then quit their manager. It may not be the manager's fault so much as these managers have not been prepared to coach the new workforce.

Managers have been trained to fill out forms rather than have high-development conversations. Only 15 percent of the world's one billion full-time workers are engaged at work. It is significantly better in the US, at around 30 percent engaged, but this still means that roughly 70 percent of American workers aren't engaged. It would change the world if we did better. What the whole world wants is a good job, and we are failing to deliver it—particularly to millennials. This means human development is failing, too. Most millennials are coming to work with great enthusiasm, but the old management practices—forms, gaps and annual reviews—grind the life out of them.

Dukes, E., 2017. Employee Engagement and Employee Satisfaction Aren't the Same. [online] Inc.com. Available at: <https://www.inc.com /elizabeth-dukes/employee-engagement-and-employee-satisfaction -aren.html>

This article considers which metric—job satisfaction or employee engagement—is the most useful for businesses to focus on, offering advice and tips to boost the latter. From the source text:

> We're all familiar with the square-rectangle logic—all squares are rectangles, but not all rectangles are squares. It's the same for satisfied employees and engaged employees. While an engaged employee is satisfied with her job, a satisfied employee isn't necessarily engaged with hers.
>
> Unfortunately, some organizations see employee engagement and employee satisfaction as one and the same. In reality, satisfaction is the bare minimum. Job satisfaction keeps employees around but it doesn't really inspire them to do more than fulfill the fundamental requirements of their role.

Mejia, M., 2016. Don't Confuse Job Satisfaction and Engagement. [online] TLNT. Available at: <https://www.tlnt.com/dont-confused-job -satisfaction-with-engagement/>

This source interprets data collected from SHRM's Employee Job Satisfaction and Engagement survey, using the numbers to explain the difference between job satisfaction and job engagement and why different tactics are needed to boost both. From the source text:

> As these survey results indicate, employee engagement and employee satisfaction are connected. But they're not synonymous. An employee can be satisfied with their pay, or the hours they work, or some of the

perks they receive from their job. But that doesn't automatically mean they're engaged. Satisfaction involves personal happiness with one's job, while engagement indicates an employee's sense of connection and commitment to advancing organizational goals.

Engaged employees are wholly interested in their work and the progress of their organization. They work hard; not with the expectation of reward, but out of an internal desire to excel in their position. DecisionWise describes employee engagement as "magic," meaning autonomy, growth, impact and connection. While employees who are satisfied—but not engaged—are pleased with what their job offers, they're indifferent about their role in the organization. They're not as invested in contributing to the company's success. They find very little, if any, magic in their work.

Rogel, C., 2018. Employee Satisfaction Vs. Employee Engagement in 2018. [online] DecisionWise. Available at: <https://decision-wise.com/job-satisfaction-vs-employee-engagement/>

This source looks at Herzberg's Motivation-Hygiene Theory as it pertains to job satisfaction and employee engagement, examining the difference between the two as well as how they work together to produce employees eager to do well in their jobs. From the source text:

Hygiene factors determine a person's level of satisfaction with their job and strongly influence employee retention. If they are not met, they lead to job dissatisfaction and cause employees to look for better opportunities elsewhere. However, the addition of more or better hygiene factors over a certain baseline will not increase job satisfaction or performance.

Motivation factors influence how a person performs on the job. When an employee is motivated, they invest more of themselves in their work and strive to do better. Merely being satisfied does not cause an employee to work harder. Additionally, an employee can be highly motivated but not satisfied with the job. They might find the work interesting and challenging, but if they worry too much about job security or think they can be paid more at a different company, they will not be satisfied. Both factors are key components of employee engagement.

SHRM. n.d. Developing and Sustaining Employee Engagement. [online] Available at: <https://www.shrm.org/resourcesandtools/tools-and-samples/toolkits/pages/sustainingemployeeengagement.aspx>

This article provides an overview of effective practices in developing and sustaining employee engagement. It includes discussion of the concept of employee engagement, its importance to business success, drivers of employee engagement, the roles of both HR and management in engaging employees, the design of employee-engagement initiatives, and the measurement of engagement through employee surveys and other communications. Global and legal issues relating to employee engagement are also discussed. This article distinguishes between employee engagement and job satisfaction; it does not address methods of developing and sustaining job satisfaction.

The term employee engagement relates to the level of an employee's commitment and connection to an organization. Employee engagement has emerged as a critical driver of business success in today's competitive marketplace. High levels of engagement promote retention of talent, foster customer loyalty and improve organizational performance and stakeholder value.

E: Further Reading on Chapter Six (Technology)

Agnihothri, S., N. Sivasubramaniam, and D. Simmons, 2002. Leveraging Technology to Improve Field Service. *International Journal of Service Industry Management,* **13(1): 47–68.**

This paper researches how technology can impact even organizations that emphasize field service, including recommendations about implementation and use strategies. From the source text:

> The primary objective of this paper is to propose a theoretical framework for assessing the role and influence of technology in creating an effective field service organization. We examine the role of technology in the context of managing relationships among the company, its employees and customers. Using the analogy of a country managing its foreign affairs, we suggest that consistent and concurrent attention to carrying out Diplomacy, Preparedness and Engagement responsibilities with the aid of Technology (DPEAT) would result in superior service outcomes. We illustrate implementing our framework in a field service organization and use a published case study to demonstrate the application of our model.

Citrix Blogs. 2019. Technology's Impact on Employee Engagement and Work Productivity. [online] Available at: <https://www.citrix.com /blogs/2019/10/30/whats-the-role-of-technology-in-improving-employee -experience/>

This article examines the role of technology in increasing employee engagement while offering direct links to additional resources to verify insight and input. From the source text:

> Organizations across industries are finding that improving employee experience leads to better engagement and productivity—and better outcomes. So what role does technology play in employee experience? Citrix recently worked with the Economist Intelligence Unit to investigate the role technology plays in employee experience. According to the survey results, 47 percent of executives said technology improves employee engagement when it provides ease of access to information.

Ease of access to information. That makes sense, especially considering that employees deal with as many as 11 different apps a day to get their work done and spend about 10 hours a week searching for the information they need. This suggests we need to balance availability of business-critical technology with ease of use and ease of access.

Coppersmith, K., 2019. How Technology Improves Workplace Productivity. [online] Business2Community. Available at: <https: //www.business2community.com/human-resources/how-technology -improves-workplace-productivity-02166853>

This article examines how technology in the workplace boosts productivity and offers detailed information about how to determine the right technology for your needs as well as the different types of common workplace technology and how they can help. From the source text:

It's no secret that technology has become a very valuable asset to any company or organization in today's business environment. The right technology can vastly improve a company's overall efficiency and performance in the market, as well as improve employee productivity, communication, collaboration, morale and engagement company wide. However, when it comes to choosing the right technology for your workplace, making the right choice can be difficult. There are numerous types of software and various tools available today. Of course, you won't need all of them, just the right ones to suit your company's needs. For example, many companies are focused on improving enterprise mobility and encouraging the BYOD (Bring Your Own Device) policy. According to research on the evolution of the mobile enterprise adoption and trends, custom apps are beneficial to both companies and their employees, with 30 percent of companies reporting custom apps improving their business processes and 24 percent of them reporting improved employee productivity, among other benefits.

Editors, F., 2017. Council Post: 10 Effective Ways to Increase Productivity Using Technology. [online] *Forbes*. Available at: <https: //www.forbes.com/sites/forbestechcouncil/2017/05/16/10-effective -ways-to-increase-productivity-using-technology/#26c665c680f8>

Written by Forbes Technology Council, this article illustrates specific ways in which technology can be used to improve workplace productivity. From the source text:

> Productivity in the business sector has been consistently dropping since 2007, according to recent Bureau of Labor statistics. Coincidentally, that was also when the modern-day smartphone rose to prominence, becoming an increasingly important part of our day-to-day lives. This begs the question, "Is the sharp decline in productivity over the last decade actually caused by technology?"
>
> While some think that banning technology can increase focus and productivity, the truth is that with some discipline and effort, the same tech can be used successfully to make most tasks simpler and faster. Below, 10 members of Forbes Technology Council explain how modern devices and applications can help everyday consumers work more efficiently, increase their productivity and ultimately achieve their business goals.

Joyce, C., J. Fisher, J. Guszcza, and S. Hogan, 2018. Positive Technology. [online] Deloitte Insights. Available at: <https://www2.deloitte.com /us/en/insights/focus/behavioral-economics/negative-impact-technology -business.html>

This article takes a more critical look at technology, describing both the benefits and likely downsides to be aware when creating an implementation plan for new or existing tech. From the source text:

> The transformative impact of technology on the modern workplace is plain to see. Face-to-face meetings have often given way to video conferences, mailrooms to email inboxes, and typewriters and carbon paper to word processors. Technology has also allowed a substantial portion of work—and the workforce—to move beyond the confines of a traditional office. It is common for digitally connected

professionals to perform some of their work in cafés or shops, at home, even lying by the pool while on "vacation."

[. . .]

In short, digital and mobile technologies give—but they also take away. It falls on talent and technology leaders to weigh the efficiencies enabled by always-connected employees against increased demands on scarce time and attention, and longer-term harm to worker productivity, performance, and well-being. Getting the most from technology and people isn't about simply demanding restraint. It's about designing digital technologies that facilitate the cultivation of healthy habits of technology use, not addictive behavior. And it's possible for leaders of organizations to play an active role in designing workplaces that encourage the adoption of healthy technology habits.

Nestor-Harper, M., 2019. The Disadvantages of Technology in the Workplace. [online]. Available at: <https://smallbusiness.chron.com /disadvantages-technology-workplace-20157.html>

This article cautions against adding too much technology at once and looks at some potential disadvantages of adding untested or unfamiliar tech to the workplace. From the source text:

A quick glance around any workplace confirms that technology is essential to business. Computer systems can run assembly lines with a few operators to monitor and troubleshoot if the system goes offline. Every desk has a computer, equipped with the latest software for data management, communications and job task completion. All this technology comes with a price. While using technology is critical to compete in today's marketplace, there are disadvantages to consider in choosing the type and scope of use.

In the next cubicle, John is conducting a job interview via Skype. Sue is walking through the office talking on her cell phone, and Carlos is into the second hour of his interactive webinar. Add these distractions to the normal noise of ringing phones, constant emails, and a noisy fax machine, and it's no wonder that it's sometimes hard to get work done. Technology demands attention. The time saving advantages are often outweighed by the constant distractions.

Newman, D., 2018. Balancing Customer Experience and Tech: Do You Have Too Much Technology in Your Workplace?. [online] *Forbes.* **Available at: <https://www.forbes.com/sites/danielnewman/2018/09/30 /balancing-customer-experience-and-tech-do-you-have-too-much-technology -in-your-workplace/#6583d1002063>**

This article takes a somewhat different approach and looks at the benefits and drawbacks of technology in the workplace as it pertains to customer experience and business goals. From the source text:

> Is it possible to have too much technology in your workplace? Experts say yes. Though it's easy to be mesmerized by the next big digital opportunity in today's market, chances are good many of us are adopting far more tech than we need—and wasting a lot of time and resources in the process. Today, the most agile businesses are working on finding the tech balance—adopting only the technology that will keep their company running strong. Below are some questions to help you determine whether your tech is in proper alignment.
>
> Does your technology support your business goals? . . . Though it's fun to think about virtual reality (VR), blockchain, and other sexy tech advancements, chances are good your company may not have a strategic use for them—at least not yet. Before you succumb to shiny object syndrome, ask yourself: what is this technology helping me do for my customers? For my employees? For my bottom line? Finding the tech balance and avoiding too much technology means being strategically selective. If you don't have good answers to those questions—show that technology to the virtual door.

Pochepan, J., 2019. How Technology Fails Employees in the Modern Workplace. [online] Inc.com. Available at: <https://www.inc.com/jeff -pochepan/how-technology-fails-employees-in-modern-workplace.html>

This source explains why technology can go wrong in the workplace when not implemented properly and offers information and tips to avoid these pitfalls while still obtaining the benefits technology offers. From the source text:

> Technology is designed to keep us focused on it. When it comes to the workplace, there are two seemingly finite resources: time and

attention. Always being connected to the office via email, or smartphones, or remote access leaves a blurred line between work and life for employees. Sure, the employee may get more done in a given day because they spend their evenings answering late-day emails, but they are more likely to resent the expectation that they have no time off to relax, recharge their batteries, and reconnect with their families. Deloitte research recently suggested there's a law of diminishing returns for the always-on employee. That employee's value is eroded by increased cognitive load and reduced employee performance and mental happiness. There is a noticeable tipping point before the employee begins to feel frazzled, overworked, and stretched too thin to perform their job effectively.

Small Business—Chron.com. 2019. How Does Technology Affect the Work Environment Today? [online] Available at: <https://smallbusiness.chron.com/technology-affect-work-environment-today-27299.html>

This article discusses the different ways in which technology can be a boon the workplace and a boost to productivity when implemented properly. From the source text:

Throughout history, technology has consistently changed the way workers across every industry do their jobs. From the industrial age to modern day, technology has improved working conditions. Its impact on the work environment has streamlined tedious and environmentally wasteful processes, expedited access to work while exponentially increasing productivity and made working from anywhere easier than ever.

Workers today are more productive than they've ever been. The impact of technology on work, both in manufacturing and in communication, has exponentially increased the rate of production and speed at which business occurs. Technology in the workplace has helped workers become more efficient than ever before. What used to take hours now can take minutes. Messages can be sent instantly to colleagues or clients across the world. Payments or proposals can be transferred almost immediately.

Ter Hoevena, C., K. Fonner, and W. van Zoonenaand, 2015. *The Practical Paradox of Technology: The Influence of Communication Technology Use on Employee Burnout and Engagement.* [online] Taylor & Francis. Available at: <https://nca.tandfonline.com/doi/full/10.1080 /03637751.2015.1133920>

This study examined the relationship between technology and employee burnout and engagement, finding that technology works to improve engagement and lower stress and feelings of being overworked. From the source text:

> Technological advancements in the workplace frequently have produced contradictory effects by facilitating accessibility and efficiency while increasing interruptions and unpredictability. We combine insights from organizational paradoxes and the job demands— resources model to construct a framework identifying positive and negative mechanisms in the relationship between communication technology use (CTU) and employee well-being, operationalized as work engagement and burnout. In this study of Dutch workers, we demonstrate that CTU increases well-being through positive pathways (accessibility and efficiency) and decreases well-being through negative pathways (interruptions and unpredictability). We highlight the importance of (1) investigating CTU resources and demands simultaneously to grasp the relationship between CTU and employee well-being, and (2) considering CTU's downsides to successfully implement new communication technologies and flexible work designs.

F: Further Reading on Chapter Seven (Optimizing Your Workday)

Cdc.gov. 2017. Worksite Physical Activity | Physical Activity | CDC. [online] Available at: <https://www.cdc.gov/physicalactivity/worksite-pa/index .htm>

This page details information about how workplace exercise can boost health and productivity, and links to a wide array of additional resources for more information. From the source text:

> A worksite wellness program that includes a physical activity component can help maintain a healthier workforce. A healthier workforce can benefit from reduced direct costs associated with health care expenses. The worksite wellness program also has potential to increase employees' productivity, reduce absenteeism, and increase morale. Additionally, these programs are often seen as a central component of an attractive employee compensation and benefits package that can be used as a recruitment and retention tool to attract and keep high quality employees. Worksites can encourage physical activity through a multicomponent approach of offering management support, physical access to opportunities, policies, and social support programs.

Edelson, N., and J. Danoffz, 1989. Walking on an Electric Treadmill While Performing VDT Office Work. *ACM SIGCHI Bulletin,* **21(1): 72–77.**

This study looks at the impact of exercise upon work productivity and overall wellness. More specifically, it examines how using active workspaces can impact efficiency and a sense of well-being. From the source text:

> The physiological and psychological health problems associated with sedentary office work are well documented, but their solution has proved elusive. In this study a specially designed office permitted the comparison of conventional word processing (sedentary condition) to word processing performed while walking on an electric treadmill at 1.4 to 2.8 km/hr (active condition). Five subjects after several days of practice produced two test trials each consisting of six 20-minute

intervals of word processing. For the sedentary condition the subjects were seated, during all six intervals. For the active condition, treadmill-walking and seated intervals were alternated. Variables measured included word processing performance score, stress and arousal indices, and body complaint count. The first of these was tested with a repeated ANOVA and Newman-Keuls post hoc, and the latter three with correlated t-tests. No significant differences were found between the two conditions for performance or body complaints. Stress was significantly lower (p < .05), and arousal was higher but not quite significant (P < .07) for the active condition. We conclude that treadmill walking, and routine word processing can be performed concurrently without a decrement in work performance, and that certain physiological and psychological benefits may result.

Lin, Y., C. Lin, M. Chen, and K. Lee, 2017. Short-Term Efficacy of a "Sit Less, Walk More" Workplace Intervention on Improving Cardiometabolic Health and Work Productivity in Office Workers. *Journal of Occupational and Environmental Medicine,* **59(3): 327–334.**
This study looked at how routine walking and physical activity improved the health and productivity of office workers. From the source text:

The aim of this study was to test the short-term efficacy of the Sit Less, Walk More (SLWM) workplace intervention. . . . This was a quasi-experimental design. A total of 99 office workers from two workplaces participated in this study. The 12-week intervention included five components: monthly newsletters, motivational tools, pedometer challenge, environmental prompts, and walking route. The comparison group received monthly newsletters only.

Generalized estimating equation analyses showed that the intervention group demonstrated significant improvements in weight (P = 0.029), waist circumference (P = 0.038), diastolic blood pressure (P < 0.001), walking (P < 0.001), moderate-intensity physical activity (P = 0.014), and total physical activity (P = 0.003) relative to the comparison group. A significant improvement in lost-productivity was observed in both groups (P = 0.003 to 0.008). . . . The SLWM workplace intervention can improve worker health and lost productivity.

Newlands, M., 2015. How Two 15-Minute Walks Daily During Work Has Increased Company Productivity by 30 Percent. [online] Huffpost.com. Available at: <https://www.huffpost.com/entry/how-two-15-minute-walks-d_b_7978520>
This article discusses how walking routinely helped to improve company productivity by 30 percent. From the source text:

> Like many companies, we're always trying to be more productive and a little bit more health conscious while at work. A couple of months ago, I read that Stanford recently conducted a survey that concludes that daily walks improve productivity and creativity, so I decided to put this idea to the test. For 30 days, we asked that everyone (if physically able) in our office take two 15-minute "walkies" (aka 15-minute walks) per day—no phones allowed. The result was a quantifiable jump in productivity of 30 percent.
>
> We track a lot of things with our employees. Engineers put down tasks, marketing has metrics and posts, finance has bills, etc. We also try to track time to complete a task. On average, each task was taking around 7 business days to complete. After we started doing our daily walks for about a week, we noticed that average dropping to 6 days, then to 5 days after about 20–30 business days of having daily walks 2x a day. Even customer service call times are down by almost 20 percent on average. While this isn't exact science, it's helped our business grow significantly.

G: Further Reading on Chapter Eight (Adapting to Change)

Hoogerhuis, M., and J. Anderson, 2019. How to Adapt to Constant Change: Create It. [online] Gallup.com. Available at: <https://www.gallup.com/workplace/268991/adapt-constant-change-create.aspx>

This source examines how change in the workplace can impact productivity and satisfaction and offers options to help make the process a bit easier. From the source text:

> A truly agile workplace culture empowers employees to think on their feet and spearhead innovation with ease. Leaders must fundamentally alter their approach to change management to create an adaptable work culture. Modern change realities require modern change strategies that prioritize the human capacity to thrive in a state of continuous change.
>
> Traditional change management focuses on processes and tools—the logistics of "what is changing" and "how it will change." Change management typically is about minimizing disruption, and it often underemphasizes the behavioral side of change. The thing is, this approach doesn't work when disruption is constant (which might help explain why more than 70 percent of corporate change initiatives fail). While processes and technology are important, the true opportunity that traditional change management misses lies in liberating people to create and sustain change.
>
> In today's ever-fluctuating work environments, the workplaces that win are home to change leaders. The ability to initiate and navigate change should permeate all levels of the company, not just the C-suite. Of course, this is a tall order—one that requires a nuanced understanding of the behavioral economics of change.

Weller, E., n.d. How to Get Past a Routine in the Workplace. [online] Small Business—Chron.com. Available at: <https://smallbusiness.chron.com/past-routine-workplace-22533.html>

This article takes a look at how making small changes to your daily routine can significantly boost your productivity. From the source text:

Sticking to a routine can help you focus and get work done. If you perform the same tasks repeatedly with little change, though, your routine can become dull, making you less productive. Bring some excitement back into your work by finding ways to move beyond or break up your workplace routine.

Index